What you chase after, you become

TYNDALE HOUSE PUBLISHERS, INC., CAROL STREAM, ILLINOIS

# BECKY TIRABASSI

# *Sacred* OBSESSION

*What you chase after, you become*

Visit Tyndale's exciting Web site at www.tyndale.com

Check out the latest about Becky Tirabassi at www.changeyourlifedaily.com

*TYNDALE* and Tyndale's quill logo are registered trademarks of Tyndale House Publishers, Inc.

*Sacred Obsession*

Designed by Stephen Vosloo and Julie Chen

Edited by Kathryn S. Olson

**Library of Congress Cataloging-in-Publication Data**

Tirabassi, Becky, date.
 Sacred obsession / Becky Tirabassi.
  p. cm.
 ISBN-13: 978-1-4143-1042-8 (hc)
 ISBN-10: 1-4143-1042-0 (hc)
 1. Spirituality.  2. Christian life.  3. Edwards, Jonathan, 1703-1758. Religious affections.
I. Title.
BV4501.3T58 2006
248.4—dc22                                                    2006016773

Printed in the United States of America

12  11  10  09  08  07  06
7   6   5   4   3   2   1

*With sincere gratitude and a deep regard for each friend*
*I have made at Tyndale House Publishers—both before*
*and after they became my publishers—I dedicate this book.*

"We are to be obsessed by God. . . . The total being of our life inside and out is to be absolutely obsessed by the presence of God. . . . If we are obsessed by God, nothing else can get into our lives—not concerns, nor tribulation, nor worries. . . . To be obsessed by God is to have an effective barricade against all the assaults of the enemy."

Oswald Chambers, *My Utmost for His Highest*

PART I

# unholy PASSIONS page 1

PART II

# public CONFESSION, PERSONAL REVIVAL page 49

PART III

# holy AFFECTION page 93

PART IV

# alone time WITH GOD page 131

# Acknowledgments

MY FRIENDS AT TYNDALE HOUSE PUBLISHERS (Mark Taylor, Bonnie Cain, Mike Morrison, and Sharon Heggeland) have been just that—my friends for many years. Since my earliest days as a youth worker, Mark Taylor has gone out of his way and encouraged others at Tyndale to help me reach students and adults with outside-the-box prayer and Bible resources. I truly acknowledge how special those efforts have been on my behalf for over two decades!

Then in the spring of 2005, a Tyndale employee, C. J. Van Wagner, prompted Mark to invite me to share at a Tyndale chapel service. (As a student, over a decade earlier, C. J. had heard me speak at a Taylor University chapel service.) At the close of a very emotional presentation at Tyndale House, Ken Petersen, senior acquisitions editor, came up to me (in front of his boss, Mark Taylor) and handed me his card, saying, "If you ever want to publish a book with Tyndale . . ."

Over time, Ken and I began a conversation that absolutely captured the passion that burns within me to tell the stories you will find in *Sacred Obsession*.

My prayer—our prayer—is that *Sacred Obsession* will draw all men and women to the One who loves them.

# unholy PASSIONS

*What you chase after, you become . . .*

*You will always gravitate toward that which you, secretly, most love. In your hands will be placed the exact results of your own thoughts. . . . You will become as small as your controlling desire; as great as your dominant aspiration.*

FROM *As a Man Thinketh* BY JAMES ALLEN

If you have little desire to be alone with God . . .

If you crave those things that are forbidden by God's Word
*more* than you

crave the things of God . . .

If you are prayerless . . .

If you are powerless . . .

If you hide or run from truth . . .

If, over time, you have not experienced increasing levels of
positive,

moral change in your life . . .

If you regularly feel more shame and guilt than joy and
peace . . .

If you read the Bible as a record of God's voice in the past,
rather than His voice speaking to you right now . . .

If your affection for God has decreased with spiritual matu-
rity . . .

If you resist sharing the gospel with others . . .

If your heart is hard . . .

If you are rarely happy . . .

If your experience with God is not personal or relational . . .

If you continually struggle with doubt and unbelief . . .

If you have no desire to help the poor, oppressed, hungry, or
hurting . . .

If you cannot *feel* God's presence, His touch . . .

If you fear people more than God . . .
Then the Sacred Obsession is missing in your life!

WHEN YOU ARE CONSUMED, to the point of destruction, by the immoral and unholy . . . and then in an instant—not through education or by preaching, but through a prayer of confession—you are consumed by the holy . . . no one can take away or diminish that experience.

It is real.

Yes, I was visibly enthusiastic when I was changed by God thirty years ago. And I am absolutely fiery about Him today! (Sometimes I am even criticized for my childlike joy in Jesus, but I don't mind . . . I certainly wouldn't trade it for a more serious or sad countenance.)

But more than that, I have evidence that there is a compelling, real Sacred Obsession that can fill your soul with more love than you could ever imagine. I have proof.

Better said, I *am* evidence. I *am* proof!

You hold in your hands my most ardent attempt to explain what I've seen, tasted, and experienced . . .

which has *indeed*

stolen my heart,

indwelled me with overwhelming emotion, and

filled me with such divine enthusiasm that I cannot stop being passionate!

The Sacred Obsession I speak of is undoubtedly the most fulfilling and exhilarating experience of my life. And this statement comes from one who has shamelessly chased after *anything* that would give me—or at least get me closer to—that elusive, satiated "high" I ached to possess. At the end of every chase, I just wanted to *feel* something. And though I chased so hard after that which I thought could satisfy me deeply . . . I always, always found it empty.

On my journey, I discovered that passion knows no bounds. Once you let it in, it takes you prisoner—whether it is holy or unholy. And during my early years, I strayed so far from the holy that I found myself on the brink of a myriad of lifeless, hopeless, passionless pursuits.

I would have never guessed, never believed, nor could I have ever imagined that I would land in a worthless, despicable, self-loathing pile of rejection. So if you are reading this and find yourself in that very place . . . I know you were never expecting to find yourself there either.

In the last year, I've put my ear to the ground and listened to hundreds of stories. Actually they are really confessions from every type of person—eighteen to eighty—of every economic status, race, and religion. And it has compelled me to write this book because I ache when I see them tasting and touching the experiences they mistakenly think will bring them pleasure.

When I consider their surroundings, educational achievements and graduate degrees, material possessions, personal accomplishments, professional positions, financial status, or well-known acquaintances . . . they *should* be happy. They should be free. They should be bursting with excitement. They should be effective. They should be full of integrity, strong in character. They should be *in love* with God. They should be—but they are not.

You cannot imagine how many people I meet who say they know God but are . . .

> broken and confused,
> hiding their true selves,
> addicted to a substance,
> involved in emotional affairs,
> extremely overweight and battling with food
>     *every day,*
> defiantly bitter about something,
> angry and easily able to wound with their words,
> abused, trapped, and desperate,
> obsessed with the illicit,
> habitual liars,

too self-centered to love those who need them, and
    consumed with chasing after the unholy.
They've believed the lie
    that the sacred is not enough.
Instead of being obsessed with the sacred . . .
    instead of loving God and others with intimacy and
        intention,
    instead of being free to dance on the inside *or*
        outside,
    instead of being able to laugh with pure joy and lift
        their hands with extreme freedom,
    instead of caring for the needs of others with selfless
        abandon,
    instead of being aware of God's presence when
        His blanket of comfort or power comes over
        them . . .
    they are numb.
That was me. Is that you as well?
Then this book is for you.

OF THIS I AM SURE: What you chase after, you become . . .
whether it is holy or unholy.

She was unhappily married. She had been unhappily married
since the beginning.

Her expectations were shattered shortly after the honeymoon. Her extremely good-looking husband was, in fact, a very troubled man. He had struggled with numerous addictions at one time, although before the marriage they seemed to be under control.

But year after year, they grew more insidious. The hiding, the manipulating, the arguing, the lying became unbearable.

Her job was fulfilling. She could smile and enjoy working with healthy people; her work was an escape from her home life. Her boss was a fine man of great character. He was kind to everyone. He was the type of man she wished she had married.

It started with a touch. Her thoughtful, sensitive boss laid his hand on her shoulder to comfort her. She brought in some baked goods for the office. He offered a bit of counsel, innocently advising her on how to handle a disappointment. She worked later into the evenings when he needed an extra hand with an upcoming project. He seemed to welcome her kind words of encouragement rather than steer their relationship back toward a professional tone.

*IF YOU THINK THIS CAN'T HAPPEN to you, think again. This is actually the story of a friend of mine. I thought it could never happen . . .*

One night they were alone in the office. She stopped by his office and sat down to visit. The peace and quiet in a normally bustling office was oddly comforting. They laughed together. The emotional tension turned sensual rather quickly. He stood up and closed the door. They embraced.

There were so many times she could have stopped the chase. But she didn't . . . and she found herself swept into a terrible trap and a shameful situation, chased and caught by the illicit.

Her life became redefined by her secret passion. Her daily schedule would revolve around their private trysts. Her mind would no longer focus on the real and urgent priorities in her life but would always be swept into thoughts of him and when they'd meet again. Others noticed that she was different, that she had become a different person in some way, distant and private.

What you chase after, you become . . .

He had hidden it for years. Not days or months, but years.

He was a leader in his community. Not a follower, but a leader. He was in charge of uniting others on the campus; he was known by all, seen as a spiritual force.

He knew he struggled, but at this point, to reveal his secret would undermine his image as a spiritual leader. He continually fought the battle in his mind but daily lost the fight to abstain. He felt shame and guilt and helplessness, yet he could not stop returning to the dark place in the late hours of the night where he would satisfy his most unholy passions.

Very smart—in fact, extremely intelligent—he was absolutely aware that living a double life would never allow him to accomplish his goals. He stayed back from the spotlight, though urged by many to step up. He could not step up because he lacked confidence; he feared exposure. The darkness was so alluring, he could not leave it for the light. Though his heart begged him . . . his mind would not stop the voyeuristic night-hour adventures.

In time, it became more and more obsessive, desiring to consume more than the dark, late hours of his nights. Even during his days, he began to think differently, his mind focusing on the illicit images and thoughts and words of his private darkness. There seemed to be no escape.

What you chase after, you become . . .

How could something so natural become so destructive?

It started simply as a quick way to melt away sad feelings. Then it became a method of controlling her environment, of becoming more perfect in her own and others' eyes. It was her way of feeling comfort. It was an unconscious way to call for help without calling.

*I DON'T TOTALLY UNDERSTAND the dynamics of every addiction, but I do intimately understand the relentless pursuit of that which gets a hold on you—almost to the point of complete destruction. And I'm guessing that you understand addictive, compulsive obsessions too. You've felt their impact on yourself or someone you love. And you know if you don't do whatever it takes to get the addiction out of your life, it will consume everything you love. Everything you are.*

Eventually it became a competition with others and even a way to feel "better than" other women. So many people would give her compliments about how terrific she looked that she strived to hear more by eating less.

She didn't see it as harmful to herself—or for that matter, to anyone else. It was her business. It was her body. It made her happy inside to feel attractive. But it took a lot of effort to eat when people were looking, without gaining weight.

At first no one noticed . . . at first. But when people began to question her about when she last ate, why she was cutting her food into such small pieces, or how much she'd eaten for lunch . . . she got frustrated with all of them. She had wanted them to notice her before—but they were too busy with their lives. And though it wasn't the kind of attention she wanted, she was starting to get attention now.

Unfortunately, it was never satisfying. Eating food or going without food produced the same result—either choice left her feeling empty and wanting more. It was a vicious, unending circle, and she could not find a way out. Debilitated, humiliated, obsessive, and compulsive, she landed in a heap at a doctor's office.

Whatever you chase after, you become . . .

HER FIRST DRINK was a six-pack, actually. She drank more than anyone else that night. And this became a pattern that would emerge over the next few days, weeks, and months. She proceeded to drink—passing out and blacking out every time she drank—all within the first few months of taking up her new social hobby. The history of alcoholism went deep into her past—father, aunt, grandfather—but it never registered with her as having any relevance or connection to her young life.

*SHE WAS JUST HAVING FUN. She just wanted to be popular.*

What started as a fun pastime grew into a lifestyle. She was certainly not alone—everyone was doing it. Everyone enjoyed a drink on the weekend.

Then she hit a car while drinking and driving. Convincing the juvenile authorities that this wasn't a habit, she talked her way out of any legal repercussions and graduated a year early from high school to get away from all the strict, controlling people in her life.

College life was exceptionally fun . . . at first. Drinking every night became a ritual. It didn't matter with whom or where or when . . . soon it was every day, not just every night. By spring quarter, she drank with the biggest of drinkers. Statistics show that girls who drink more are more likely to be involved sexually. And she was . . . although not intentionally. At first it was innocent teasing, but later it turned into almost being gang-raped. That was enough of a scare for her to leave school . . . but not to stop drinking.

Nightly drinking escapades almost always turned into sexual encounters . . . first with dates, then with friends of friends, and finally with strangers. It eventually took its toll. One addiction turned into another—drugs entered the picture. And a downward spiral into shame and self-hate and depression, aided by anesthetizing drugs and alcohol, ended in another, more serious car accident, a hospital visit, and a court hearing—all by the age of twenty-one.

What had begun innocently enough as an athletic, smart teenager's desire to lead a fun, exciting life had become—in only six short years—a sad, suicidal-plagued existence hanging by a thread. Chasing after alcohol had turned her into an alcoholic.

What you chase after, you become . . .

I KNOW THIS TO BE TRUE because this last story is my story.

I chased after a "high" to escape the pain of my reality. I found it first in one substance that led to another and ended in a combination of drugs and alcohol. My thirst for excitement still unquenched, I pursued security and love by living with a boyfriend. To get to deeper places and higher highs, I had to turn away from what was good, true, and right to chase after what I thought would make me happy, fulfilled.

*OF THIS I AM SURE. What you chase after, you become—whether it is holy or unholy.*

I made intentional decisions to chase, pursue, go after what I wanted. But to do so . . . I had to leave my family, experiment with the forbidden, and risk my reputation. All to possess what I thought would fill my needs for pleasure and excitement . . . anything that would make my nerve endings tingle . . . and make me *feel* passion.

THOSE OF US WHO WIND UP in a heap at a doctor's office, in a court hearing for doing something illegal, or ostracized from our families because we've shamed them don't ever really *think* about where the chase will end. In fact, it is as if we consciously choose to turn off the part of us that thinks . . . to follow that which feels.

Perhaps you don't buy the idea that what you chase after, you become.

Then just look at how much time you spend doing it, or even more telling—how much time you spend thinking about it, strategizing, manipulating or hiding the truth from others, even lying in order to protect . . . your very own unholy passion.

Perhaps there is a lie you do buy? You believe you are entitled to chase after that which you think will make you feel alive—full of real, living, passionate feelings.

But *you* know, just as *I* knew, that these things or persons—pornography, illicit sexual relationships, greed—don't make you more alive . . . they make you numb. They actually *steal* from you. They steal your joy, your peace, even your money! They *use* you. They *take* from you. Eventually (sooner, rather than later) they will ruin your reputation, smother any affection you might have for God, and ultimately destroy your purpose for living.

These things take *you* from *you*. They change you—they transform you—into what you are chasing!

Alcohol transformed me into an alcoholic. What a shock, eh? Yet I could not see it or identify myself with it. I refused to believe it possessed me. I would not call myself by that name . . . because I did not want to give up that which brought me a certain measure of escape and pleasure . . . though oh, so temporary.

I honestly believed I would miss out on something exciting or soothing or sensual if I stopped drinking. In reality, I was attempting—hourly—to escape, hide, and anesthetize my pain. I thought I was chasing after pleasure, but I was really running from pain.

It's crazy. It doesn't make sense logically, but by the time you are consumed by something, you don't think logically. Others can see you acting stupid or placing incredible importance on something unrealistic. Others can see you reaching for nothing or protecting your right to something so insignificant, yet to you—it is worth losing everything for . . .

Take pizza, for example. There is no need whatsoever to eat a whole pizza—or to eat more than a few pieces. You can always buy another pizza tomorrow. But most of us, alone with a pizza—a really good, tasty, cheesy pizza—find it almost impossible to stop eating when we are full. Yet the initial satisfying taste in our mouths eventually turns into a full, too full, upset stomach from the very same pizza that we loved at first bite.

*PERHAPS YOU DON'T THINK you are chasing after that which is dangerous or even deadly.*

Same with a drug, a forbidden relationship, a vile image—they seduce us with their promise of pleasure, only to take us to a place of remorse and shame. Yet remorse and shame are not enough to stop the repetition. We come back for more . . . though we know how it will end.

Can you see? We are all enticed toward that which is forbidden—the illicit, the immoral, the unholy. They are determined to have a strong, strange hold on anyone who will give them attention. They almost have a voice. And as they call you to come to them, deep inside there is another voice begging you not to listen, not to pay attention.

MY WITTY, BRILLIANT YOUNG PASTOR recently taught on the subject of Money, Sex, and Power, challenging those of us in the infamous OC (Orange County, California) with this question, "What has your affection and attention more than God? Is it money or sex or . . . ?"

In Orange County, known by the rest of the country as the destination in which you can fulfill the most tantalizing of materialistic or even scandalous pleasures, he was certainly touching on our reality. We do have a reputation as being a county full of youth-seeking, pleasure-driven, power-hungry, ultra-thin, sun-worshipping, ageless, recreation-loving residents.

He then had the guts to call the objects of our affections "rival gods."

For most of us, it was a shocking, almost rude interruption into the selfish lives we find ourselves living . . . our hearts could not help but be stirred . . . to consider looking at life from a different perspective, other than . . . "what I want . . . what I need . . . what I deserve . . ."

WOULD YOU, FOR JUST A MOMENT, consider what— *or even who*—might be the rival god you are cherishing—the unholy passion that lures you away from the holy?

Perhaps you still don't think you are dabbling with unholy passions. In fact, if you were honest with me, you might admit that the word *unholy* makes you a bit defensive. Maybe even angry.

You adamantly believe that what you so tightly hold onto,
    what you possessively cling to,
        what you jealously guard as your own . . .
isn't really wrong. You don't see it as an obsession, or an

addiction, or even a problem. You simply consider it a bad habit. You are certain that what you are doing isn't hurting anyone else. You contend that you are in control of it . . . yet your actions and thoughts suggest something different.

Might I sincerely offer you a bit of vital information? Receive this, please, from one who . . .

has been to the other side of many addictions . . .

has become way too familiar with most unholy passions . . .

and was eventually consumed with the illicit, illegal, and immoral.

*THERE IS AN INCREDIBLY MYSTERIOUS, powerfully insidious seduction in the pursuit of the unholy that pursues you and me—— endlessly.*

I AM GUESSING YOU KNOW it as intimately as I do: There is some real (or perceived) pleasure in the world of the unholy, some measure of escape from emotional and even physical pain. But there is *also* deceit and distress and even hatred—especially toward oneself. Though it might creep up on you gradually, there is a juncture—a turning point—when the unholy begins to rapidly overtake and over-whelm your body, mind, and soul.

At this juncture the need for more of it outgrows your ability to satisfy it with a fix. Eventually, the desire grows so strong that at times, it seems as if it is consuming you, sucking the life out of you . . . until there is no way out of the dark, secret, shameful place . . . but death. You actually consider death. You ponder whether it would be better to die than to live your life . . . this lie.

Your mind is consumed with one recurring mantra: "Take your life. You are worth nothing now. How much longer can you hide who you really are? . . . You know you cannot change. Only shame awaits you if you expose how you live, what you do, who you love."

This, my friend, is the nature of the unholy. It is determined to take you captive. And it is patient. However long it takes, death *is* its goal and end.

Some of you, like me, will foolishly hold out hope until the very end, believing that you can somehow get control of your unholy passions. And if you wait too long, you will get caught or humiliated or publicly shamed. Cherishing—hiding—sin in your heart only leads to extreme paralysis.

UNHOLY LIVES ARE INAUTHENTIC LIVES; they are full to overflowing with deception. You fear being caught. So you hide the truth. You rationalize. You reserve the right to hold on to your secret. You still want an option to use, touch, feel, and relapse . . . to possess the unholy—but it really possesses you.

No one *ever* thinks they'll get too deeply involved or overly consumed in something dark or wrong or bad . . . or sinful.

*SOME PEOPLE CANNOT—or perhaps, will not—call themselves sinners. The label seems so despicable. If you want to possess the sacred, then calling sin "sin" is nonnegotiable. This admission, this identification, is the beginning of the end of your unholy passions.*

If you have opened your heart to the unholy, you will soon close your eyes to the deception involved. But if you can still hear the plea of a sojourner who once loved sin and found it empty, please hear me say, "It cannot save you; it cannot satisfy you completely; it is not your friend. It is a stealer, a killer, a destroyer. It seeks to own *you*. It has a nature, a purpose, and a passion to possess you. It cannot love you. It hates you—and it hates the holy."

Instead, I know only one way to be free from it— whatever or whomever it is. Run from it. Hate it. See it as the poison it is—as the home wrecker, the liar, the inauthentic, the fake.

HERE IS THE TRUTH about unholy passion.

I recently spoke at my church. We are a group of over four thousand Orange County residents, most under the age of twenty-seven . . . who are chased by and chasing after . . .

In an emotionally heartfelt plea, I suggest that there *is no* proven, systematic, manageable approach to maintaining self-control over the unholy. Oh, I contend, you might be able to temporarily silence the unholy lusts and temptations of your heart, but they lie in wait like an animal lurking for prey, ready to pounce and devour you when you least expect it.

I am relentless to expose and challenge . . .

*THERE IS ONLY ONE WAY to win over the unholy. You must kill it. Remove it. Mortify it—or it will mortify you.*

My voice begins to intensify as I ask each listener to end his or her chase after the unholy passions of his or her heart.

Sincere passion doesn't meet a lot of resistance.

I can feel the temperature change; something melts. I can feel hearts softening; there is no defensiveness filling the room. Instead, I see hope-filled tears well up in people's eyes. Young men and women move closer to me, edging up in their seats. They look right into my eyes to see if I am telling them the truth.

When you hear someone passionately tell you that you can really stop—*in an instant*—the addiction, the lies, the double life, the guilt—everything in you wants to know the way to such a freedom! They, just like every audience who hears this word, are desperate to know how, when, where.

My invitation is not a private offer, though; it is public. I always say, "Come forward. Come now. Run toward the holy God . . . relinquish the unholy passions in your life." And at each service, without exception, it is the men who are first to their knees.

Most memorable was a very strong, athletic student. As if just in off the beach, in a ball cap, T-shirt, sandals, and board shorts, he startled me as he stood up and charged toward me. Then, just as abruptly, he dropped his face into his hands and fell on his knees by my feet. He sobbed so loudly and his shoulders shook so hard that everyone in the front two rows could not help but notice him. We were magnetically drawn into his pain, his confession, his remorse. We could not help but cry with him.

I received his tearful confession. He stuttered and mumbled and begged God to help him to quit using, to stop lying, to end the madness . . . he named the sins that he had so easily adopted and that were now consuming him.

Holiness. That's what he wanted. He wanted to be free of the all-consuming hold that the unholy had over his thoughts, his actions, and his relationships.

Isn't that the picture of everyone with whom Jesus personally meets? The woman at the well . . . the prostitute . . . the tax collector. He barely mentions sin; they each knew what it was in their lives, and they hated it as much as He did. But suddenly, His love melts their hearts. They know they must choose . . .

ON A RECENT FLIGHT, I sat next to a woman who was reading a book called *A Sequel to Sex and the City*. Having my own opinions about the prevalence of sex in every city, I was curious why she chose to read this book. To understand what compelled her, I asked, "Did you read the first in the series"— I filled in what I assumed was its title—"*Sex and the City?*"

"Yeah," she replied in a dull, monotonous tone. "It wasn't very good."

I said, "Oh . . ."

I didn't really know where I was going with this, but I tried to get a conversation started by asking another question. "It was about . . . ?" When she didn't seem to have a reply, I quickly filled in the blank. ". . . about . . . sex in the city?"

At that juncture I thought we'd both be embarrassed, but she wasn't. She replied, "Yes, it was a quick read—rather entertaining."

*Entertaining?* I thought. I wondered whether you read a fantasy to be entertained, or to fill a void of loneliness in your own life through fictional sexual escapades. Besides, doesn't it seem futile to read the sequel if the first "sex" wasn't very good?

*THERE IS A LOT OF sex in the city to partake of these days. In fact, there is a lot of sex in the city even for those who don't want to partake of it!*

When my son, Jake, was in his early teens, he and I were flopped on our stomachs, sprawled over two queen-size beds high above the city in a hotel tower, waiting for friends to join us for the evening. In typical fashion, we had been pitching the remote control back and forth across the room, taking turns surfing the channels, looking for familiar sports, movies, or entertainment shows in an unfamiliar town . . . when one of us happened upon a pornographic *something.*

It took us both about two seconds to realize we were watching something vile. By the time I dove for the remote control and found the up or down button, we were laughing, blushing, and gasping in shock and embarrassment.

I have never been able to shake from my mind the image of what I saw on television that day. It was foreign to my eyes, unthinkable as an act of love, and—unfortunately—unforgettably disgusting.

Yet I was as curious as much as I was repulsed. The lure of the illicit was so intense I wondered how I would have responded if I had the tiniest inkling of attraction to such a pornographic scene.

Pornography is initially intense and incredibly alluring. And once it grasps your curiosity, hooks you—as far as I can see and from everything I've heard—it keeps reeling you in until you are caught.

AT A RECENT CONFERENCE, I spoke as a writer . . . a first for me. I shared how my personal commitment to prayer, purity, and purpose has influenced each book I've written, most recently *The Burning Heart Contract*. I love relating the story about Henrietta Mears and Bill Bright in their early college-ministry days—how they, along with two others after an all-night prayer meeting, committed themselves to what they called "Christian discipleship" in the following tangible forms:

1. Spending no less than one hour in prayer and Bible reading each day

2. Complete sobriety
3. Chastity (sexual purity)
4. Sharing Christ with at least one person
   each year

THE RESULT OF THEIR BURNING HEART commitment was to issue a call to over eighty college campuses during the next two years. It resulted in a well-documented revival across American college campuses from 1947 to 1949.

For me, the story had both personal and vocational impact. When I first heard the story of the 1947 Fellowship of the Burning Heart, I too had been praying for one hour a day for almost two decades. For even longer, I had maintained sobriety and fidelity. And for all but two months of my Christian life, I had shared the Good News as my occupation or vocation! Upon finding the story tucked away in Bill Bright's biography, *Amazing Faith,* I considered myself an honorary member of the Fellowship of the Burning Heart. More importantly, I felt compelled to reprise the Burning Heart call and extend it to students and adults in the twenty- first century.

I contacted Vonette Bright, my friend and Bill Bright's widow, to discuss the idea—which she was excited to endorse. In October 2004, I hit the road with the message, but I had no idea how much prayerlessness, pornography, sexual immorality, sexual-identity issues, and alcohol abuse I would find among those *of all ages* who called themselves Christians.

*"IF I WERE YOU, I would make the prayer meeting a special feature of my ministry. Let it be such a prayer meeting that there is nothing like it within 7,000 miles. Somehow we must keep up the prayer meetings, for they are at the very secret source of power with God and with men."* —Charles Spurgeon

Whether I'm speaking for a couples' retreat, for a singles event, for writers or for students, I issue a Burning Heart call. And at each meeting, I have found one prevalent struggle that has beset the average American Christian. Based on my unscientific but very consistent research, sexual addiction is a serious problem for . . .

students from every part of the country,

those who are ministers of the gospel,

single adults, and

married couples of all ages.

When I offer to pray for and receive the confessions of others, I am no longer shocked by the number of men and women who share how their lives have been negatively impacted by pornography. It is becoming the norm rather than the exception.

Viewing sexually explicit and illicit Web sites is consuming, ruining, and possessing . . .

the young and old,

the married and single,

the unbeliever and the believer.

It has no boundary—no respect for age, occupation, or marital status. What often starts as an innocent curiosity within a very short time becomes a compulsive fetish, an unstoppable fascination, a dark secret, a true addiction of incredible proportion in a person's life. And as much as I've traveled and as often as I've mentioned the subject, I have discovered that this addiction is a stronghold in the lives of far too many people! So I've just started calling it out, naming it. And I offer to pray for people who want to confess it as sin and be free from it. . . .

At this particular writer's conference, a woman my age was the first to reach me. She said, "I had been married almost twenty years when I discovered that my husband was addicted to pornography."

Frankly, I wasn't surprised, but I was curious why she had come up for prayer. She seemed compelled to report to me, "I'm married to a new man now."

I thought to myself, *Oh, I guess that first marriage didn't make it?*

But she surprised me when she continued, "My husband got help five years ago. After much healing in his life and in our marriage, we've started a ministry to men in our community that addresses the issue of sexual addiction, specifically pornography. Becky, the reason I am coming to you today is to tell you that we've ministered to over seventy-five men to date. *Without exception* every man who is currently addicted to pornography started the practice at the age of eleven or twelve—*without exception*! You have to keep doing what you are doing—calling students to get help now before they carry their addictions into their marriages."

I prayed with the woman and couldn't help but remember a college senior who had the guts to stand in front of his peers at one meeting and say, "I've been addicted to pornography for six years—and I've been married for the last two years! It doesn't go away when you get married. If you need help, get into a men's group now. There is hope and help right now, right here on our campus."

Not one week later, while sitting in a church, I was handed a letter from a woman who had heard me speak about pornography. She wrote, "Keep talking about this, Becky. I am married to a man who forces me to use pornography in our marriage bed. He feels that it is appropriate. It is shameful to me . . ."

IT APPEARS that the struggle of for most Christians is no longer alcohol or drugs or smoking—those addictions have vir-
tually faded in comparison to the devastation of
pornography, illicit sex, immoral sexual relationships, and
other sexual fantasies.

So I don't avoid the subject; I just tell it like I see and
hear it. Pornography is consuming the young, the old, the
married, and the minister.

Yes, I do mean the minister. It isn't often that a minister
feels safe enough to speak publicly about this struggle, but on
one particular evening, the floodgates were opened and dozens
of men and women in ministry honestly and transparently confessed their struggles with pornography, emotional affairs,
even sexual identity. They were full of guilt and shame and
fear—but my words to them were no different than the words
I share with students: Confess your sins to one another so that
you may be healed. Leave your sin at the altar. Don't return to
it. Become accountable to a counselor and a small group of
people with whom you can be honest. If necessary, put software on your computer to keep you from "using," change jobs
if necessary, end the improper relationship . . . come clean.
And stay clean one hour, one day at a time.

SEXUAL ADDICTION is prevalent, powerful, and pervasive on
most college campuses, in many homes, and in every com-

munity. Maybe it is because of the Internet. Who knows? Who cares?

God cares. It is idolatry. It is self-satisfaction. It is worship in the truest form. It steals purity. It corrupts the mind. It humiliates marital love. It projects a false reality. It thwarts any chance for intimacy with a holy God. It is sin at the deepest level—both flesh and spirit are destroyed in its path.

YOU ARE NOT ALONE if you find yourself consumed by the unholy. Unholy passions will forever fight to consume you. They never stop.

Because I so publicly share the power that my sinful charades had over me, I am also a frequent recipient of tearful confessions and emotionally draining admissions from those Christians who are stuck, lying, cheating, hating, pretending, using, and dying from their love of unholy passions.

And this is the norm, not the exception. This is what I hear almost everywhere I speak. Everywhere I go, I meet those who call themselves Christians but who are sin plagued, sin stained, and full of shame. They are stuck in the wildly alluring pursuit of the illicit, driven by a compulsive addiction to want more of whatever gives them temporary pleasure, and completely oblivious to the pain they are causing themselves or their families, their coworkers, or their God.

Can you see the dramatic irony in this? Those who profess to know and love a holy God are, in fact, chasing after the unholy with more zeal and fondness than they ever, ever felt toward Him.

This is a life-and-death issue.

The unholy never ends in life; it always ends in death.

IT IS ONLY A MATTER OF TIME before sin delivers death—to dreams, health, relationships, security, sobriety, peace . . . even life itself. And if losing life isn't enough . . .

Your unholy passions humiliate the holy God who loves you. When you are willing to see and feel His pain and the shame it brings to His name, you will be compelled to turn from sin and run toward life. But even if you won't relinquish the unholy, be sure that the unholy hates you and will use you to humiliate a holy God.

*YOUR HEART INSTINCTIVELY KNOWS how to keep itself from God's searchlight—the Holy Spirit and the Word of God. If you let your heart rule your life, it will valiantly fight to keep you away from truth— distracted, disinterested, unbelieving . . .*

I know you want to live and not die, to be really alive, fully and passionately alive. The Holy Spirit of the living God wants to dwell in you, creating true, lasting, eternal life . . .

but He will not—indeed He cannot—share space with the unholy. Your life is a battleground between the holy and unholy. You must choose.

Do you know, can you believe that you were created for God? Can you see how the unholy wants to disfigure you? To mar, mark, and disable you? The holy and the unholy fight over you—but One fights for you because He loves you. The other, because he hates you. You are so valuable—you are worth fighting for . . .

IF YOU WILL—ONCE AND FOR ALL—mortify (slay, hate, kill, and destroy) your rival gods, those unholy passions that separate you from God and others, then you will *feel* new. You will be free to chase after—with endless passion and true abandon—the most sacred obsession that your heart can desire. I am absolutely convinced that if you turn your well-honed passion for the unholy into an equally zealous pursuit of God . . . who indeed desires to be the object of your most intense affection, to become your most sacred obsession . . . you will end the inner war and find peace.

There is only *one* Sacred Obsession.

∞

WHEN IT WASN'T AS TRENDY and popular as it is today, I was a binge-drinking college student. I drank until I got drunk—

and I drank every day. I smoked pot *and* two packs of ciga-rettes every day. I swore profusely and could tell the most disgusting jokes. I was the kind of girl you drank with in college, not the kind of girl you dated. I truly thought my party lifestyle was very normal for a fun, athletic girl; I kept up the pace, even though I blacked out and passed out nightly.

From the time I entered college, the drugs and alcohol became more and more frequent. I'd often miss class or wake up in someone else's room after an all-night party. One night, I narrowly escaped being sexually assaulted by an entire rugby team. Rather than admit I had a problem, I dropped out of college *the next morning* and returned home without even saying good-bye to my friends or roommates.

But I didn't quit drinking. Why? I'm not sure . . . per-haps I *couldn't* quit drinking.

For many of us who grew up in the Midwest, a trek to the West Coast seemed like the best way—if not the only way—to find a new life. At nineteen years old, I wanted adventure. So I took off with girlfriends to find the endless excitement the Beach Boys promised—partying with beauti-ful people on magical, tropical, sandy coasts overlooking stunning sunsets upon the endless waves of the bluest waters. And I wanted . . . a surfer boy to love.

I abandoned all common sense to get it. I proceeded to

do everything I'd said, as a young woman, I would never do. My appetite was insatiable for anything risky, fun, or promising a high.

I was able to consume *more* of any substance—alcohol or drugs—than most people. I was also willing to get it illegally, and I was never afraid of potential negative consequences. I was oblivious to any danger, and I refused to stop using . . . for anyone or any reason. What at one time would have repulsed me—things I'd have seen as sleazy or trashy or filthy—had now taken hold of every fiber of my heart and body.

I was high for more hours in a day than I was sober.

On my twenty-first birthday—that very night—I did two things . . . I quit smoking cigarettes, and I moved in with a guy whom I had met just a few weeks earlier. I was an all-or-nothing kind of gal.

By this time, I didn't like anything about myself when I was sober so I just stayed high . . . all day long. Speed in the morning, pot during the day, scotch on the rocks after work, wine before bedtime. Day after day after day . . . and I loved my life. I did.

*IT NEVER, EVER crossed my mind that I was an addict.*

That summer, I returned home to Ohio to be in a wedding. I was honestly looking forward to seeing my "old" friends and the "old" life I had left behind a few years earlier. I sincerely believed my California life was enviable—my boyfriend was really cute, I was completely in love with him, and I was certain we'd get married. I even had a good job. What more could a twenty-one-year-old girl want out of life?

The night of the bachelorette party, I did what I always did—I drank with my friends. But in an old, familiar place, my point of oblivion came much earlier than usual. There was no limiting mechanism in me.

I woke up the next morning in bed with a man I barely knew.

You can just imagine my first thoughts . . .

*What did I do with him? What if I'm pregnant?*
*How will I tell my boyfriend what I've done?*

But it was an honest, gutsy self-reflection that really hit me hard.

*You would never have done this if you hadn't been*
*drinking.*

THAT WAS THE FIRST DAY in six years I said the words *I'm an alcoholic.* I was sick to my stomach. I couldn't eat or sleep, *not* because I was hungover, but because I was so afraid of the consequences. For the first time, I knew that I was not going to be able to get out of this situation without a lot of personal humiliation or great losses. I didn't even consider the difficulty I would incur upon withdrawal from alcohol.

But, for the first time in my young life, I was determined to quit drinking.

Three days later, I returned to my California life. It was only a few short days before my mind and body were racked with the emotional meltdowns and physical shaking and trembling that addicts often experience. I tried to go through this withdrawal without telling anyone what I was dealing with . . . until I couldn't take it anymore . . . I became so conflicted, suicidal. Even though I wanted deperately to quit drinking, I couldn't.

I awoke one morning and instinctively I knew I wasn't going to last one more day. My boyfriend was coming home in a few days from a two-month vacation, and I would have to tell him that I had cheated on him and that I might be pregnant—and I would not know by whom. Then I would have to tell him that I was an addict. We had always enjoyed drinking together, but I knew he would be surprised—if not ashamed—to hear me call myself an alcoholic. Surely he wouldn't want me anymore . . . and that petrified me. I was so afraid to lose him.

What had for so long been my comfort, my companion, had become my enemy. Alcohol consumed *me*— instead of the other way around . . . Alcohol had stolen every dream . . .

You would think I could hate it and run from it. But I couldn't. It had me. It was all I could think about. And when I couldn't stop thinking about it . . . the compulsive thoughts turned into suicidal thoughts. My pursuit of adventure and desire for love had turned deadly. I just wanted to end my pain; I decided I would rather die than face the consequences of being an alcoholic, losing my boyfriend, and having a baby.

That same morning, I had to appear at a deposition. An entire year earlier, I had hit a car while drinking, and now I had to face the owner of the other car and representatives from both of our insurance companies to discuss the accident.

This was just too much for me. I couldn't face another day, another consequence, another problem.

I gathered enough courage to attend the deposition . . .

Before entering the conference room, an assigned lawyer sternly reminded me that if I lied and the case went to trial, I'd be crucified in court.

Lie? I *lived* a lie. I was a liar, a drunk, an addict, someone who slept with strangers . . . I was disgusting, even to me. I vividly remember feeling so ashamed of myself that I could barely look anyone in the eye.

For many reasons, not all of which made sense, I felt

alone. I could not see tomorrow. I was hopeless. This is a terrible, horrible place to find yourself.

The lawyer's word, *crucified,* began to filter through my mind, over and over, giving me a picture of something from my past. I had been a churchgoing kid—like most Americans in the 1950s and '60s. I had been baptized as a baby, confirmed in junior high, and required by my parents to go to church every single Sunday until the day I left home at seventeen. There was only one person that I knew of who had been crucified . . . Jesus Christ. Finally, into my tossed-and-turned-about mind, came a single thought: *God loves you.* And . . . hope slipped into my heart and mind. I could feel something or Someone giving me different thoughts—telling me *not* to commit suicide, *not* to give up on life, *not* to be afraid, *not* to run away . . . telling me that I was *not* alone . . . until I finally realized it was true. *I was not alone.*

I left the deposition after telling the truth—at least all I could remember, which wasn't much—and I drove . . . not toward home or back to work, but to a church.

I drove there with the intention of finding someone who could help me.

LOOKING BACK, it was a classic scene. A disco-dancing, miniskirted, platform-shoed alcoholic drives into a church parking lot to find someone to talk to, and when she finds no one upstairs, she runs down a set of outdoor church steps, only to find the church janitor.

In fact, the only human being at the church that afternoon was the janitor. He was buffing the floors. He was wearing work boots, blue jeans, and a flannel shirt. He didn't have a classroom or a pulpit. He had a janitor's closet. And that is where I found him.

By this time, I was so confused and crying so hard, I had no idea what to ask, what to say, how to explain my shameful life . . . but it didn't seem necessary. Somehow, the janitor knew what I was looking for . . . and he knew just what to say.

"We have to pray," he said. "Do you *want* to pray?"

My answer still surprises me. I was an addict who lived with her boyfriend. I was the last person you'd find in a church! But I hadn't felt so safe in a very long time. I didn't even feel out of place; in fact, I felt as if I was coming home. I simply replied, "Yes."

I was twenty-one years old, and I had lost more, given more, and thrown away more of what most people treasure—purity and respect—and I had no expectation that I could get any of it back; I was just hoping to stop the madness. I did not want to live this out-of-control life anymore.

The janitor asked, "Do you want to ask Jesus Christ to

come into your life?" It makes me smile to rewrite this account—because I knew right then, at that moment, everything was going to change. My life was out of control. Why not let go of it and give it over to God? It seemed so right, my only option—and such a breathtakingly simple idea!

Odd, don't you think, for me to be so distant from God yet so unafraid to ask Him to come into my heart? Actually, I wasn't being fearless, I was being a child who wanted a parent to lift me out of the hole I had dug for myself and fallen into . . .

*YOU CAN'T HELP BUT TELL the story of when your heart was captivated by real love. You'll gush. You'll beam. You'll be radiant. And frankly, others will either want what you have, or they'll be ticked off that they don't have it.*

What followed was the most transparent, honest confession I have ever made in front of another person. The janitor asked if I could think of any sins . . . I often laugh when I recount this part of the story because there were so *many* areas of my life that were full of trouble, I knew he'd be shocked! Yet I didn't defend myself at that point. Was I a sinner? Yes, of course, I was one who was consumed by sin. In fact, I did not resist being called or calling myself a sinner. It was obvious. But the janitor knew how to restore my soul . . . and to this day, I am so very grateful for his confident, calm direction.

The janitor encouraged me to confess directly to God anything that I knew of in my life that was not true or right or pure. Well . . . he was very patient to receive every tearful, specific confession I had to give. I was compelled to get rid of these forbidden holds over my life, strangling thoughts, and destructive addictions.

With each sordid, seamy admission of sin against God and others, I felt an immediate release of guilt. So I held nothing back. And with each and every dark place I exposed, I began to *feel* new feelings—good ones. I could *feel* love coming into me. I began to calm down. I laughed with joy, releasing more and more of my pain—all between tears of humiliation and sorrow. The desperate feelings were leaving, and I was feeling happy, unafraid, even forgiven. I knew I didn't deserve any of these incredibly wonderful emotions or feelings. Most importantly, the new feelings weren't going away. They were growing more powerful by the minute, completely obliterating and overtaking the suicidal and hopeless thoughts.

*WHAT WILL SUSTAIN true, unending, overflowing, moment-by-moment holy passion? Confession.*

﹀   The janitor then asked me to renounce the devil by
exposing any interaction I had with the occult. For some reason, this didn't bother me or sound weird. I didn't have a
long list, but whatever I could think of, whatever came to
mind, I named and renounced. And just as quickly as I asked
God to forgive me for dabbling in those things, I received
another soul shower . . . clean, fresh water washing away the
filthy dirt inside of me.

The sequence of prayer began by asking Jesus to come
into my heart in the same simple words a little child might
utter, then admitting—out loud—absolutely every sin I
could think of . . . and believe me, this went on for a while.
I then renounced the devil, using the service often used at a
baby's baptism, which we found in a hymnal in the classroom
next to the janitor's closet.

As if offering me a final piece to my prayer, the janitor
suggested that I ask the Holy Spirit to come into my heart,
my inner being, and fill me up. So I did. But I didn't just
say, "Fill me." I asked for more, all, as much as I could get
of the Holy Spirit! And with the very same enthusiasm with
which I drank—consuming more than anyone else—I experienced a filling up to overflowing with an extra measure of
the Holy Spirit. I was ecstatic! I was joyful. I was empowered. I was happy. I felt strangely out of my own control
yet safely within God's strong and holy presence.

I was wildly excited about telling others what had just happened to me . . . even though I wasn't really sure what had just happened to me! I did not feel, look, or act like the same person who had run down the steps. I was new, and I knew it. The old Becky was dead and gone—good riddance, eh?

*NO, I'LL NEVER BE THE SAME. I'll never see or love or talk the same way I did before I met Jesus. Oswald Chambers says, "Once you have seen Him, you can never be the same."*

Within the next twenty-four hours, I quit drinking alcohol and taking drugs, moved out of the apartment I had shared with my boyfriend, and stopped spewing filth with my filthy mouth—even though no one asked me to do any of those things.

I immediately quit chasing my unholy passions. I had no more interest in pursuing them. They held no more intrigue for me or power over me. I instantly hated them— what they did to me, how they lied to me, what they stole from me.

What I could not give up for months and years before meeting the janitor . . . was gone in one day. And with the very same obsessiveness I had invested in unholy passions, I began to chase after the holy.

In a little church basement, I found both adventure and love—exactly what I had hoped to find in California.

I AM CONVINCED that you, too, can have a "janitor" experience with the living, loving God. But there is a change of heart that is critical. You must forever see your unholy passions as worthless, sickening, and utterly shameful. You can no longer hold onto them, hide them, or love chasing after them.

You and I instinctively know how to chase after what we . . . want,

    need, or

        think we deserve.

I believe that our "inner passion pursuer" has a switch that can be flipped. We can wholeheartedly pursue either the unholy or the sacred. Sometimes it takes sheer force to flip the switch. Other times it takes complete release of any control. Many times it requires that we stop believing a lie and follow after truth.

When—*if*—you obsessively chase after the holy with all your heart, mind, and soul by repeatedly soaking in the always-present and all-powerful Holy Spirit of the living

God, you *will* possess all of the sacred . . . all of the time
. . . to the demise of anything and everything unholy.

*"EACH OF US is as full of the Spirit as we really want to be."*

——*J. Oswald Sanders*

It doesn't matter who you are or how old or how smart
you are . . . whether a student, an addict, a parent, or a pastor—if the unholy is being safely harbored in your life, you
must instantly, immediately turn from it, then determine to
hate it forever *if you want to be free from it*. If you *want* the holy
to enter into your life and stay, then . . .

Don't believe the lie of the unholy passion that pursues you!

Don't live a life without pure passion!

Don't chase after what will never satisfy!

Chase after the sacred. Chase with the same enthusiasm,
the same tenacity, the same insatiable appetite you have
when you truly want something . . . and I promise you, in
the pursuit of the holy you will find more passion, emotion,
freedom, happiness, and power than you can ever imagine.

# public CONFESSION, PERSONAL REVIVAL

*As the open confession of my sins to a brother insures me against self-deception, so, too, the assurance of forgiveness becomes fully certain to me only when it is spoken by a brother in the name of God. Mutual, brotherly confession is given to us by God in order that we may be sure of divine forgiveness.*

FROM *Life Together* BY DIETRICH BONHOEFFER

AFTER THREE DAYS ON THE ROAD, I boarded my sixth flight and cozied into the middle seat with a new book.

In the aisle seat next to me was a professor from a Northeastern university known for its diversity and liberal politics. Her brief introduction made me smile . . . we were quite opposite in just about every way. And we quietly spent the next few hours in our own worlds. As soon as she started grading papers, I opened a book written by an eighteenth-century theologian who had briefly been the president of Princeton—Jonathan Edwards. My friend and former boss Jay Kesler, the past president of Youth for Christ USA and president emeritus of Taylor University, had just given me the book a day earlier.

As a board member of my newly formed nonprofit organization, Burning Hearts, Inc., Jay was meeting with me to discuss what I had seen and heard as I put my ear to the ground on college campuses during the past year. Almost three decades earlier, I had begun my life's work with students as a volunteer and eventually a staff member in the organization over which Jay presided as president. My youth-work days had come to a close at least five years earlier, but most unexpectedly I found myself unable to do anything but return to college campuses and call students and leaders to return to revival—to be sold out to prayer, set apart in purity, and sent out with purpose. Perhaps the most fascinating piece of this puzzle was finding such a receptive audience to this "Burning Heart" message.

During our lengthy breakfast meeting, Jay and I had been swapping stories for quite a while when he asked if I was familiar with the writings of Jonathan Edwards. I had often quoted Edwards; I certainly knew who he was, but I had not read any of his books.

Jay suggested that what I was experiencing and seeing and hearing was very similar to what he had read about in Edwards's book titled *Religious Affections*.

I hadn't yet mentioned to Jay the title for this book, *Sacred Obsession*. The title had been chosen months earlier during a brainstorming session with my editor. Now, the similarity of the two book titles took my breath away. I wondered what likeness might lie in two books so *obviously* focused on passion and faith, yet written centuries apart by two *obviously* different people.

Jay became convinced that I should not leave Upland, Indiana, without a copy of the book, as well as George M. Marsden's extremely lengthy biography, *Jonathan Edwards: A Life*. He was *so* insistent that I wait while he raided his personal library that I began to sense something significant was at stake—there was something very important for me to discover within this book. As the divine push continued, Jay added one, two, three more books to my pile of reading—much to his wife's and my surprise. Yet another title especially caught my eye. It was a treatise written by John Owen—an author and thinker who was almost a hundred years ahead of Edwards's time. *Sin and Temptation* was stuffed in my carry-on luggage as well.

Over the next few flights, I couldn't put the Edwards book down. I was deeply moved with every page of *Religious Affections*—mostly because it captured both my earliest and current experiences with God. In so many ways, it validated that my initial experience with God was the reason for my continued, endless passion for Him. It was exciting to read the centuries-old essays by a renowned theologian. He explained how everyone could and should experience a lifetime of excitement and exuberance toward God—and not because of religious education or service, but as a result of affection toward *Him*. And though I have often felt that some consider me shallow, emotional, or childlike, I know I am happy and in love with Jesus—a most vital test of true religion, as Edwards would say!

*WHAT GOD REVEALED through a brilliant eighteenth-century theologian strangely warmed this twenty-first-century woman's heart. More than that, it may have ignited a bonfire!*

I was having a fabulous experience with God while reading *Religious Affections* thousands of feet in the air. With each page, I uncovered simple but eternal truths available to anyone who truly wants to know and love God. Edwards maintains that the path to God is most passionately pursued . . . and most voraciously obsessive . . . when our love for Him is the reason for our pursuit of Him. Edwards says we receive God's love through the heart, not through the mind or intellect. He suggests that when our hearts need and receive forgiveness—especially when we know we don't deserve it—we will be forever loyal to the One who forgives us, even to the point of danger, exclusion, or rejection by others. He encourages his readers to love God with all their feelings and emotions.

I eagerly read, took notes, highlighted, underlined, pondered, and smiled for four hours.

During that time, my seatmate and I spoke very little; we certainly did not discuss politics or religion. We made only brief quips about the drunk across the aisle—who was incredibly annoying. Then, just as the airplane touched down, she asked what I was reading.

I had been deeply immersed in a rousing epistle about loving God! How could I explain, in a few short minutes, what a powerful impact this 250-year-old book was having on me? But I tried anyway . . . and she listened with great interest. Even with all our differences, there seemed to be no barriers between us. She was genuinely captivated by the sincere explanation of my relationship with God and my love for Him. In less than five minutes I told her my janitor story, how my former boss gave me this centuries-old manual, and how it so wonderfully inspired me to write my book for a new generation.

AS A SPEAKER, you hope to connect with every audience—even those with whom you have very little in common. So as a white, middle-aged, Midwestern woman within minutes of entering a room 90 percent Asian, I knew I was going to have to work to find that common ground. I was not at all familiar with Asian culture. But the audience was primarily college-aged students, so I trusted that they would respond to my passionate call to prayer, purity, and purpose in the same manner that most other students responded—with personal revival that started with Spirit-led conviction and culminated in any necessary lifestyle or character changes.

But about thirty minutes into my talk, my brow started sweating. Nobody was even nodding their head up and down, affirming what I was saying. (This is never a good sign for a speaker.) I could tell things weren't going well, but I didn't know *exactly* why. Maybe I was tired? Maybe it was too warm in the room?

At the close of my talk, I couldn't seem to shake the feeling of disconnection, so I blurted out, "Can anyone tell me what God said to you tonight?"

Silence.

Complete silence.

I started to sweat even more. Yet I couldn't believe that not one person in the room had sensed any conviction or passion or insight. So I asked again, "Nothing? God said nothing to you?"

One smiling young man in the back of the room quickly raised and then lowered his hand, shouting out something, but it wasn't loud enough for me to hear. When the students around him started to snicker, I called out to him, "What did you say?"

This time he yelled loudly, "We're Asian!"

Now the whole room laughed aloud—except for me.

I said, "What does that mean?" (Mind you, this is a large group meeting . . . )

He said, "We don't really like to share in public. We'll talk to each other later."

"Oh, okay," I replied. "Well . . . " Thinking through what, if any, impact this information would have on my overall challenge to them, I continued, "I'm *still* going to ask of *you* what I ask of *every* audience. If God has shown you something tonight, something in your life that you must let go of or get rid of or confess as sin, I'm going to ask you not to leave this room as the same person who entered. Because God is looking for those who are ready to be used for every good work; He is looking for those who—as it reads in 2 Timothy 2:21—will keep themselves pure, special utensils for honorable use."

With a little lump in my throat, I asked the students to take the next twenty minutes during the worship time to consider their response. I mentioned that I would sit on the left side of the room if anyone wanted to pray with me.

Only one student moved . . . at first. But it was intentional. He was up and walking with the first strum of the guitar. I was surprised that such a strong and confident-looking young man would be the first to sit next to me. And without hesitation and very little emotion, he began to share.

"You talked about pornography tonight. You told about a man who had been trapped in it for ten years . . . well, so have I, and I'm only twenty-one. I'm sick of it. I can't get my head and my heart to come to the same place with it—I can't stop it and yet I hate it and I know, most of all, that it is keeping me from doing those things God wants me to do."

We talked for the next twenty minutes, then we knelt together and prayed. Then I encouraged him to buy filtering software for his computer before the night was over. I also asked him if he had someone with whom he could be accountable for sobriety over the next ninety days. And finally, I asked him if he would be able to come to the prayer meeting the next morning. He was open to each of my suggestions but he regretted that he would be unable to attend the morning meeting because he had a previous commitment.

Three hours later, I was still sitting on the left side of the room, receiving the confessions of these very dear, shy students. It didn't seem as if the meeting should end quite yet. But the building's alarm system was going to be activated at 11 p.m., so we left the room at 10:58 and stepped outside into a light drizzle. I still didn't think the meeting was really over, so I asked if anyone wanted to go out for a cup of coffee.

*DON'T HOLD ON TO YOUR SIN. Don't hide it any longer. Call it by its name. Don't minimize it. Don't deny its power over you any longer. Confess your sin to another . . . so that you may be healed.*

Only two guys and a gal remained. We drove over to the coffee shop . . . and that's when I realized that I really didn't know Asian culture.

The confident young man—we'll call him Jim—was still hanging around, and he made a point of telling me, "God changed my morning plans, and I will be able to attend the prayer meeting." I didn't realize then how integral he would be to the entire campus prayer effort.

Jim asked if I wanted to get something to eat at the "Asian Ghetto." Having no idea where the ghetto was or what I would get to eat at it, I said, "No thanks. How about you go there and come back with your dinner?" We both laughed.

He took off, and now just one other student was sticking with this white, middle-aged woman.

We made small talk for a few minutes . . . until twenty-five students who had been at the evening meeting flooded into the coffee shop along with Jim. They had been at the Asian Ghetto—which turned out to be an Asian food court near campus. When they heard I was having coffee around the corner, they came over to tell me, in person, what God had said to them during that meeting.

Oh, my heart jumped—it was burning up with a deep love for these students and for God! It was so fun to hear each of them share their sincere insights and convictions. It lasted so long that we had to move our "meeting" over to the empty hotel lobby, which was conveniently located next to the coffee shop. Into the wee hours of the morning, we formed a big circle . . . and one by one, in quiet conversation, each student shared something very personal. They were patient to listen to each other. They were not afraid to speak the truth about their lives. Some shared honestly about how difficult it was to make time for prayer as busy students.

Others talked boldly of the desire to see revival on their campus. Many confided about their struggles to remain sexually pure. But all of them expressed how much they wanted to live passionate, holy lives. They wanted to be ready for God to use them. Wow . . . Wow.

As our time came to a close, I said, "I will never forget this night." The students had been so transparent and honest with me, and I learned so very much about each of them and their Asian culture. They were extremely passionate and sensitive and respectful. They beautifully articulated their love for God and were willing to learn more about prayer from a new friend. After a closing prayer, I simply said, "Thank you for inviting me into your lives and making me feel so special."

The next morning, about sixty students who wanted to see revival on this very large state-university campus showed up to learn more about prayer . . . and before the morning was over, Jim stood up and asked his peers to do something radical on their campus—to join together for forty-eight consecutive hours of prayer for revival.

Within three days, through Jim's focused leadership, they had secured a room, acquired furniture, set up a Web site where students could sign up, and gathered over 150 students to pray. A riveting power surge had been released on their campus when these students began to understand the relationship between prayer, purity, and purpose. And true to collegiate form, an extensive blog documented their forty-eight-hour journey for all to read.

∞

WHAT LASTING IMPACT has *Religious Affections* had on me?

Among other things, it's helped me understand the importance and power of confession.

Confession brings healing.

The degree of shame and false guilt that men and women try to hide until they finally act out enough to be seen and heard is ridiculously unnecessary. God has given us a path toward healing in James 5:16: "Confess your sins to each other and pray for each other so that you may be healed."

What is the holdup? Fear of exposure, loss of respect, removal from authority? Well . . . maybe you should be exposed and removed, but it doesn't mean you can't find healing and hope and restoration for a new life in devotion to Christ.

You can defeat sin's domination over you with one sincere, public confession. There is transforming power in public confession. It forces your head and your heart to agree.

I USUALLY ARRIVE the night before I speak on a college campus. The next morning, I am picked up and dropped off by some warm body at the venue where I am to speak. On one particular crisp, fall morning, I arrived at the auditorium thirty minutes before anyone else entered the room. I didn't need the extra time, so I relaxed in a chair and reviewed my notes.

Then with one quick comment, all my expectations for the morning changed. A lone student had sauntered into the room and nonchalantly mentioned that today was prospective student day.

*Hmmm . . . sounded official . . . but what did it mean to me?* I wondered. She went on speaking, as if answering the question I never asked, saying, " . . . parents from all over the region will be attending the morning chapel."

I thought, *What?* Parents? Parents! *My talk is not for parents! It's for students!* I came prepared to talk straight about what I see and hear on college campuses—alcohol abuse, pornography, sexual immorality, and lack of fire for the living, loving God. I was going to lay it all on the line, and the presence of parents would undoubtedly change the atmosphere and receptivity of the students to my message.

My options?

None. There was no time to regroup.

Within seconds, well-dressed parents began streaming into the room along with their neatly dressed high schoolers . . . in addition to the very casually dressed campus residents. *What a diverse group,* I thought. *None of them has the same interest or agenda in being here today. What a conundrum!*

Before my brief introduction, I was trying to catch the chaplain's eye with a wide-eyed look, as if to say, "Hey, thanks for the inside scoobie!" But it was too late and it didn't really matter. By the time I was on my way up to the platform, I determined to give the very talk I had planned earlier that morning.

So I prefaced the talk by saying, "Parents, you're not here. Students, parents are not here. . . . I came here today to ask you, students, if you have a burning heart for God."

As always, I started with the janitor story—which is shockingly blatant about sex and drugs and alcohol.

At one point, I said something that always, always gets a big laugh—and no one even chuckled. That's when I knew the parents were still making their presence known . . . so I mentioned this fact to them. That was enough to let the tension out of the room, and finally everyone laughed.

"There are three kinds of hearts," I said . . .

"*dead* hearts—dark . . . never even lit,

"*dim* hearts—their passion for God has faded; something is smothering their fire, and

"*burning* hearts—sold out, set apart, and sent out for God."

I gave it my best effort . . . encouraging, challenging, and sharing from the reservoir of uncontainable passion within my own burning heart. Then I asked, "Which heart do you have? Which heart do you want?"

At the end of my talk, I asked the students to raise their hands if they wanted to let go of that which might be quenching or smothering their fire. I asked them to stand if they wanted to fuel the fire in their hearts—into a blazing flame—by making decisions to spend time with God, *daily* talking to Him and listening to Him. Then I invited the students to come up afterward to talk with me, to pray, especially if they would like me to be their "janitor."

I really thought very few students would make any strategic moves . . . the atmosphere just wasn't conducive. But at least thirty students raised their hands, and another thirty kids lined up—some with their parents—to look into my eyes and tell me they had made some type of decision that morning.

About thirty minutes later there were five people left in the room . . . two women and two students . . . and me.

The first woman asked her daughter to wait in a seat

while we spoke. Through tears, she softly asked, "Would you be my janitor?"

IF YOU PUT YOUR EAR to the ground for even a very short time, you, too, will hear the stories of those who have been chasing the unholy and are ready to pursue the sacred. You may hear more than you want to. But it is a sign of the times.

IT IS TIME FOR CONFESSION to do its work and bring us back to . . .

> the place
> of receiving the simple forgiveness and healing
> we *need and want*
> in order to move away from the sin that has stolen our
> passion for the Holy One.

THE POWER OF PUBLIC CONFESSION was never more evident than when I suggested to one thousand students in the Northwest that I had observed a pervasive spirit of pornography over many young Christian leaders across America. I shared that I had heard more private confessions of sexual addiction in the last month than I had heard in a lifetime before that. I begged the young men and women to see the lie that had invaded their hearts and minds and culture.

I simply spoke the truth: "Impurity steals true intimacy with God and others. If you are addicted to pornography, you are creating a false expectation for marriage, and you're worshipping vile images—and that is just the beginning of the end."

As I began to close the meeting, the young man who had been the MC for the evening walked up to me on the platform and picked up a microphone—unannounced and uninvited. Not so privately, in front of one thousand students, I whispered, "Do you want to say something?"

He said, "Yes."

I asked, "Now?"

He replied, "Yes."

"All right . . . " I reluctantly—and blindly—conceded.

He spoke powerfully, not timidly, and with indignation. "I'm the very leader that Becky has just described. I've been addicted to pornography since I was twelve years old. I'm tired of losing the battle. I'm ready to fight. If you want to fight this battle with me, meet me tomorrow night in my dorm lobby at 7 p.m."

Many young men poured out of their seats and came to the front of the room, falling prostrate on their faces . . . without anyone even asking them to do so.

I KNOW THE POWER of unholy passions and how difficult it is to come before God and others to pour yourself out in confession to them.

So when I speak, I speak as a sojourner, as one who has herself been consumed by addiction, as one who has lusted after the gratification of the flesh.

I know compulsion. I know addiction. I know self-destruction as intimately as anyone on the face of the earth. I almost lost all my faculties—and my sanity—to an addiction to alcohol and drugs. I have given over my body to the immoral and illicit.

I have chased the unholy and found nothing but pain and shame at the end of my chase.

So at any and every meeting—however long or short a time I am given to speak—I tell my own and others' shameful stories and then I offer the unbelievably simple choice for change: confession. Turn, I say. Kill, mortify, leave behind that which has consumed your life—the idol, the lust, the person, the substance, the addiction, the secret. I name as many of the idols and addictions as possible.

IT DOESN'T MATTER what you chase or worship or love . . . if it isn't God, it will always lead to destruction of body, mind, and soul. Always.

I can tell you with authority what it feels like to see and hear and taste everything once you are in the light. I know what it feels like to unload one's shame on another person whose only response is to take your hand and put it into the hand of the One who will set you free. I know the thrilling, breathtaking adventure that begins immediately when you enter the land of the living.

I feel as if I can sincerely, powerfully, confidently take your hand and put it into God's hand. He will help you step out of the dark.

So I offer the opportunity to anybody to change their lives in a moment . . . come forward, come clean, come and stay in the light, I say.

Then I close my eyes and wait for people to respond to God. In most places, I open my eyes to find more kneeling men and women than there is room for them to kneel. In my whole life, I've never seen what I have seen in the last year. Men—of every size, age, and economic status—run down the aisle and fall to their knees, sobbing. Women—young and old, who are tired of living double lives, full of sexual compromise, when all they want is true and lasting love—come and kneel.

I pray with men and women in ministry who are so wrapped up in secrets that they cannot speak through their tears. I pray with students who are outspoken leaders at the beginning of a meeting but later divulge the greatest of addictions when given a safe place to do so. I am honored to be that "safe place" for them. And though I don't know them and their situation personally, I am confident that it only takes one transparent moment, one sincere and humble prayer to change one's life for eternity, even—or perhaps especially—if you are sharing that moment with a relative stranger.

At the impromptu request of my young pastor, I bounded onto the band's platform to share about the forty days of prayer for revival on college campuses that I was beginning in a few days—in front of about a thousand students at the Sunday evening video service.

The idea to call students across America to pray consecutively for forty days had come over me almost unexpectedly. It was a culmination of my visits to college campuses the previous year, which had created in me a great need to call students to prayer. Yet I had no platform or venue from which to advance this concept.

God's idea quickly became clear and was very simple: Set aside 40 Days of Prayer for Revival on College Campuses. Call everyone you know—students and campus ministers alike—and invite them to be a part of forty consecutive days of twenty-four-hour prayer.

So I did. In less than a month, the forty days were assigned to state, private, and Christian colleges that each agreed to fill twenty-four, forty-eight, or seventy-two hours with unending prayer. How and where they would set up their prayer rooms would be unique. But they would invite their fellow students to pray in dining halls, libraries, chapels, classrooms, or apartments—and I would visit each campus to encourage them and symbolically pass the "prayer baton" from one school to the next.

I took off on January 20, 2006, on a tour of college prayer rooms—most built from scratch for twenty-four hours; others, remodeled prayer chapels that had existed for decades—turned into twenty-four-hour prayer rooms, now full every hour of the day with on-fire, praying students.

As I excitedly listed off the twenty-plus schools that had already signed up for the forty consecutive days of prayer, I had a little agenda. Two of the local universities had not signed up, and I was hoping to spark some interest in any students from their campuses. I gave the announcement—then my pastor asked me to pray a "prayer of release" for those in attendance to receive the message the preaching pastor was going to deliver.

Coincidentally, I had spent the day re-reading a book by

Wesley Duewel titled *Revival Fire*. It is full of revival reports and also quotes renowned Christian leaders such as Charles Spurgeon—one who taught preachers how to preach in the mid- to late-1800s. Tucked into the book was the strong charge made by Spurgeon that the pastoral prayer was the most important part of every service. In fact, if he had the choice, he preferred to pray for the people, rather than preach to them.

So when the pastor, without warning, invited me to pray for the congregation, I took the responsibility seriously! I immediately switched gears from "announcement giver" to "pastoral pray-er" and brought the congregation with me to a place of kneeling before the King—asking for His presence and for the immediate outpouring of the Holy Spirit. Then I sat down.

I took notes during the sermon, and when the time came for response and worship, Communion and confession, I sat a while before getting up to leave the room.

As I arose, a praying leader stopped me by calling my name. I looked at him, and he said, "This young woman needs a woman with whom to pray." I thought, *OK*. Switching gears again, I settled into being a praying leader. There was no room to pray where we were, so I suggested that we step into the Communion station a few yards away.

As she began to speak to me, I watched a man in his thirties approach me. He could see I was in the middle of a conversation, yet he tapped my shoulder to interrupt me. He was persistent—as if he had been looking just for me.

I looked at him and frankly, my first impression was *Where did he come from? He can't be a regular here . . . he's dressed too nicely.* I wasn't being judgmental; it's just that our church—70 percent under the age of twenty-seven—is characterized by casual, flip-flop-wearing, blue jeans, T-shirt, or sweatshirt-and-ball-cap kinds of students. So when the starched-white-button-down-shirt-and-dress-khaki-pants fellow with Italian leather shoes approached me, I sensed that he was a first time visitor.

I stepped aside so that he could speak privately to me, and he said, "I'd like to confess my sins." I looked at him and thought, *What part of that announcement or that sermon caused you to come up to me and ask me if I would take a confession of sin?* Nothing I could think of, nothing that made any logical sense. That is when I realized—I'm slow, I guess—that the Holy Spirit of the living God draws men and women whenever He wants, wherever they are, to meet with Him.

I asked the man to give me a minute to conclude my conversation with the young woman . . . to wait at the corner.

When I finished, I found him kneeling, waiting.

I asked, "Are you Catholic?"

He said, "I was raised Catholic. I went to Catholic schools—through college."

I thought I could understand his progression. He was coming to the Lord after years of being away. He knew his life was full of unconfessed sin. He was ready to confess it, but even more so, to enter into a personal relationship with God in a new and powerful way.

I asked, "Would you like to ask Jesus to be the Lord of your life—to come into your heart? Do you want to confess your sins, as it says in James 5:16, so that you may be healed?"

He said, "Yes."

I shared a bit of my janitor story, then I asked if he wanted me to be his janitor. He said, "Yes." This was the easiest conversation with a seemingly strong, confident man that I could ever recall having. . . .

I had the sense that God had been working on this man's heart to a point of breaking . . . the breakthrough was here, now; the Lord had guided him through his years of religious training back to Himself. It would begin with confession.

I said, "I'll open in prayer, but then you speak to the Lord from your heart. Confess out loud the sins you came to confess to the Lord. First John 1:9 says, If we confess our sins, He is faithful and just to forgive us our sins, and to cleanse us from all unrighteousness'" (KJV).

I took the man's hands, bowed my head and closed my eyes, and began to pray. "Dear Jesus . . . come into my heart."

He took over. He began to genuinely talk to Jesus, asking Him to forgive him. He confessed specific sins, and with each one, he squeezed my hands tighter and tighter. (I was cringing from the pain of my wedding ring being pressed against my knuckles!) His sincere, strong, unabashed confession led to a release of power in his life—as I witnessed it.

He finished praying, and we looked at each other. We were standing near one of the many Communion stations located around the room—where a cross and the Communion elements waited for you. So I just pointed to the cross—and he smiled. He smiled so big, so wide. He was free and clean. He was full of the Holy Spirit and emptied of unconfessed sin. He was excited to take Communion!

New start. Fresh wind. Great power. New life in Christ.

Public confession. Personal revival.

*THAT'S REVIVAL, ISN'T IT? When the Lord visits your soul . . . when the healing or convicting presence of the Holy Spirit is felt and heard without a word being spoken.*

I find that once a person's life is consumed with . . .
    hidden and unconfessed sin, or
        the darkness of soul that begins with believing lies
            and often leads to depression, emotional unrest,
            physical pain, even unto desperation . . .
                breakthrough often comes with a dramatic,
                personal touch from God.
At one college, we began with about eight hundred
students for a time of worship at 7 p.m. Then I shared
some words of encouragement through storytelling, and
afterward opened the meeting for a time of prayer and
worship. This naturally flowed into a time of open-mike
testimonies.

By the third hour in the same room, only about a hundred
students were left. . . . Even though many had left, the worship songs remained sweet, and the many students who
remained to pray became more transparent and more sincere
as they drew near God through confession and petition. I
determined to stay in the room until there were no more students who wanted to pray. . . . During the fourth hour a shy,
young woman stood in front of me. She said, "I was going to
commit suicide tomorrow. In fact, I was going to meet with
my counselor for our weekly meeting and then commit suicide
afterward."

In a split second, I recalled how I had tried *not* to fly to that school on that particular day. My schedule was packed, and I'd really wanted a short time at home between speaking engagements. But there seemed to be some unknown, pressing reason for this school to arrange for me to come on that specific Sunday. In that moment, I understood. Tucked randomly into an already-booked semester chapel schedule, Jesus had a divine appointment. He knew just when, just how, just where He would meet this young woman.

I looked right into her eyes and could share only one thought with her. "Jesus is here for you tonight. Jesus has been waiting for you to come to Him tonight."

*RIGHT BEHIND YOU a voice will say, "This is the way you should go," whether to the right or to the left. —Isaiah 30:21*

We prayed together, and then I was able to bring an administrator into our conversation. Together, we followed the appropriate steps to help this young woman—that night, into the next day, and through the next month. The timing seemed so critical . . .

I am convinced that God personally met that young woman's emotional needs that night in that room. He was there to save her life. He had her safely in His care . . . a suicide was aborted that night.

A PHYSICAL HEALING was also received that night.

As I proceeded to pray with students who had every imaginable need, one young woman came up to me and said that she had had a severe problem with her spine since high school. She had numerous operations and was always—daily—in pain. She felt during the service that God wanted to heal her.

I am one who believes in healing because I received a healing. I will always pray for the healing of another; I will almost always ask God for a physical healing—though I know it is up to God how, when, and in what way He will answer that prayer.

So I prayed a simple prayer with this young woman. About two weeks later, I received an e-mail from a faculty member who shared that this young woman had stood up in chapel at the invitation of an administrator to share her experience. She had been pain free and without medicine since the Sunday-night meeting!

But the story doesn't end there.

Six months later I was sharing with a small group of campus ministers about the revival meetings I had been holding. Near the end of an hour and a half of sharing, a woman started to cry. She was visibly upset, but it wasn't clear why.

It took her quite a while to share the entire story, but she began by saying, "I'm just putting two and two together. You're the woman who prayed with my daughter. She had numerous spinal operations that have never brought healing to her body. In fact, she has rejected further operations because of the excruciating pain. As a mother, I have watched her suffer daily . . . until attending a Sunday night Burning Hearts meeting on her campus. She told me that during the meeting she felt God wanted to heal her, and she came up to a woman to pray.

"It has been six months since that meeting. My daughter is a different person—she doesn't take medication and doesn't live in pain anymore."

∞

PSALM 34:11-22 SAYS:

> Come, my children, and listen to me, and I will teach you to fear the LORD. Does anyone want to live a life that is long and prosperous? Then keep your tongue from speaking evil and your lips from telling lies! Turn away from evil and do good. Search for peace, and work to maintain it. The eyes of the LORD watch over those who do right; his ears are open to their cries for help. . . . The LORD hears his people when they call to him for help. He rescues them from all their troubles. . . . The righteous

person faces many troubles, but the LORD comes to the rescue each time. For the LORD protects the bones of the righteous; not one of them is broken! . . . The LORD will redeem those who serve him. No one who takes refuge in him will be condemned.

THESE VERSES, IN MY OPINION, speak of revival. The word *revival* is itself something of a lightning rod; it is almost a divider of camps. Why do some people want it while others do not? Here is my take . . .

*Revival has a cost.* The cost is holiness. What does holiness look like? I think it is best summed up by the psalmist: "Turn away from evil . . . "

When we are ready to pay the price of holiness—not for a season, but as a lifestyle—to live and love a holy God, then no one and no thing will be able to stop revival!

Revival is the nonstop river of life flowing from our being; so convincing, so healing, so hope filled, so loving and forgiving . . . it will change the course of our nation.

What might revival look like? Parents will humbly, sincerely go to their children and ask for forgiveness; they will make restitution and amends. Ministers of the gospel who need to do so will repent and confess, so that they may be healed and so the work of the Lord can be released in their churches. Students will shake off their compulsions *daily, hourly*—they'll hate what they used to love and love what they used to hate. All, and I mean *all,* will consecrate their lives and service afresh to the Lord . . . *and then* we will see revival.

Revival is when you and I are consumed with talking about, living for, praying to, worshipping joyfully, and greatly loving Jesus every day—all day! It is contagious. It is fun. It leaves you fired up. More importantly, I discovered this: Revival ends when . . . you want it to end.

I've been in "revival" and on fire a long time—since August 26, 1976, to be exact—and I don't plan on revival ending in my life when a twenty-four-hour prayer room is dismantled or when the 40 Days of Prayer for Revival on College Campuses ends . . . I didn't go to campuses to encourage prayer meetings because I need them to keep me on fire for God.

I am convinced that revival is you and me living in the supernatural power of the always-present, holy, and awesome God—right where we are. And if there are enough of us, it will start a bonfire for the Lord Jesus Christ.

*PRAYER IS THE COMPONENT that sustains any revival— personal or corporate!*

It is possible to be in a revival all your Christian life. So whether you are one little flame of a fire walking on a very dead campus . . . or you are the only one in your home or workplace who is a pray-er . . . you must never let the fire for God get dim or die out in your heart.

Revival is a never-quit proposition. It carries a with-or-without-you mentality within its core. It isn't a meeting or a string of services. It is a fire, a passion, an unquenchable faith.

Revival people are praying people—they know their God, and their God knows them.

Revival people love the Word of God, read it often—always—daily—and live by its standards, not by the standards of their peers, pastors, or parents.

Revival people listen to God's marching orders . . . they respond, they act, they do not quench the Holy Spirit; they do not procrastinate when God gives them their marching orders. They do not fear man.

I guess it makes sense why some people want revival and others don't.

BEFORE I BEGAN the Burning Hearts ministry, I had never been to a "revival" meeting—if you can believe that—even though I had been a Christian for over twenty-five years. I just had never attended a church or worked for an organization that used that term to describe any of their meetings, services, or speaker's series. I'm serious. So when I told my

thirty-five-year-old pastor about this "new thing" that was
burning in me, he suggested that we have one—a *revival* for
all those in our church between the ages of eighteen and
twenty-six—for four days!

Four days? I was taken aback by the thought. I had been
considering calling students to prayer, purity, and purpose.
And the idea of meeting with the same students for four
nights in a row seemed to open up limitless options for that
message to unfold.

*IN MY WHOLE LIFE, I've never observed more spiritual effort exhibited
than during those four nights of meetings.*

We even discussed, at length, the use of the word
*revival*. My pastor was concerned that the word might have
different meanings for different people—and some of those
meanings might be worn so thin that the word could lose its
emphasis. So we found a compromise that worked for all of
us. We determined to call this revival "Burning Hearts:
*Return* to Revival."

The work actually began six months prior to the meetings. A handful of us started meeting weekly to pray for God
to visit us in power during those four days. Then, for seven
days leading up to the meetings, a larger group met each day
at noon to pray in the center where the meetings would be

held. And a few days before the meetings, an incredibly creative group of volunteers created a prayer room that possessed almost a coffee-shop atmosphere in which students could receive prayer at any time before, during, or after the messages.

It was the prayer room that was packed for up to four hours every night. In fact, students lined up outside the door, each night—all night long—just waiting for someone to pray with them, to hear their confessions or concerns . . . to anoint them with oil. The classroom-turned-confessional contained small, round tables with softly lit lamp candles centered on them and two chairs placed at each table. The room was framed with large swatches of black linen draped over room dividers to add a feel of confidentiality to each station of prayer.

I encouraged students to follow a suggestion Henry Blackaby had given during a meeting I attended the previous month. He said that whenever the Holy Spirit touches you or convicts you of sin—at anytime during a service—you should get up out of your seat and "do business" with God immediately. Don't even wait one minute!

Though none of us was really familiar with this procedure, hundreds each night found comfort, forgiveness, and power in the prayer room. The evidence continued well after the meetings, as we received testimony after testimony describing the life-altering healings and revelations that had occurred during those times of confession and prayer with elders, life-group leaders, and pastors in that room.

My husband was one of those camped out in the prayer room each night. He, along with each praying leader who volunteered to be in the room, saw the mighty ministry of the Holy Spirit firsthand. Only after debriefing the first night with him did I understand the power of confession.

Having never been a part of a revival, I was looking for feedback on the entire evening. But my husband replied, "I never heard a word or a song. I was in the prayer room for four hours. There were people lined up outside the door the entire night, waiting for someone to pray with them."

We were exhausted after four nights of Burning Hearts, but we agreed we had never seen so many people ask for prayer in our entire lives. Our view of ministry had changed. Everybody who entered a prayer room was changed. Everybody who made decisions with the will and mind was changed.

IN THE MONTHS leading up to this, my first revival meeting, I began exchanging books with students from Azusa Pacific University. They had become my fellow sojourners in the "school of revival." First, I dusted off and read a book from my own library about Hudson Taylor's life—it was enthralling to grasp how deeply Taylor loved God and how passionately he served Him, even at the expense of health and comfort.

I began to voraciously acquire and read books about the lives and ministries of those who had experienced revival, such as D. L. Moody and John Wesley. But it was the book that a student gave me that really lit my fire . . . and has kept it burning.

Charles Finney compiled a record of the revivals he held during the nineteenth century and titled it *Lectures on Revival*. This four-hundred-page book (with very tiny print!) contains every important insight Finney gained from his revival tours: the troubles, the obstacles, the people, the prejudices, the breakthroughs, the signs, and the excitement. It especially confirmed to me that what I was seeing, feeling, and experiencing was not something new, but something old—something called revival.

I also recognized some of the obstacles Finney had encountered during his meetings—people who were afraid of confession and what it might uncover . . . even the lack of desire for revival to come!

But most important, I found confirmation in his writing that revival is about confession and cleansing, not about roof-lifting-off meetings. It is about tears and remorse and the personal realization that God is holy and, in general, we are not! Finney tells story after story about the moral change of entire communities, of how individuals known for their immorality would publicly and willingly give up their unholy lifestyles. He described the faces of people changing in front of him; he watched people's love for God grow exponentially—and their love for self rapidly diminish. He saw ministers' lives change as well.

He saw, led, and taught that a true revival will create a shake-up in most lives. And that is what I was seeing, everywhere I gave the simple message God had put on my heart for this time and this generation.

God is calling us back to Burning Hearts . . .

1. to be sold out to prayer—to reserve time for Him alone every day when we might pour our hearts out to Him and listen to Him through our daily Bible reading . . . when we might allow Him to search us, convict us, empower us, and speak to us.
2. to be set apart in purity—willing to be holy, live holy, and reflect a holy God; to turn from anything that we chase after that is unholy, both as individuals and as a community.
3. to be sent out with purpose—not only to understand that He created us with a purpose in mind, but to joyfully serve Him with our lives (our talents, gifts, and possessions) now and forever; to be so revived in our personal lives that we are involved in concerted

efforts that result in fulfilling the great commission—
a great awakening.

AS I'VE READ the works of some of these great revivalists, I've
noticed something they all have in common: Confession and
conversion were absolutely nonnegotiable traits in every true
revival. Whether in the presence of one person, four people,
or hundreds . . . the relinquishing of sin, whether of the flesh
or the spirit, was a precursor to the release of God's power
upon a person or a community.

*"GOD IS DELIGHTED to empower us as often as we need Him, and we
need Him more often than we realize. We have become too
complacent and too easily satisfied with minimum manifestations of
His power."*—Wesley Duewel

John Owen wrote, "There is not a duty we perform for
God that sin does not oppose. And the more spirituality or
holiness there is in what we do, the greater enmity to it. Sin
never wavers, yields, or gives up . . . no area of one's life
indeed is secured without a struggle."

Perhaps one of the most powerful moments of response I
have ever had as a speaker was shortly after I finished reading
Owen's book *Sin and Temptation*. Upon quoting him to an
audience of over four thousand men and women, mostly

under the age of thirty, I felt as if I had disclosed a well-kept secret to a desperately-seeking-for-truth crowd. It was as if they knew it but had never heard it—sin sought after their "saved" souls, and they would have to fight against it all their lives in order to stay free and far from it!

Complacency would kill them. They knew it. Flirting with sin would destroy them—if it hadn't already. A simple truth exploded over us like a fire-sprinkler system spontaneously letting loose on an entire room of people.

By the hundreds tears were shed. Confessions were made. Forgiveness and hope were received. Ears and eyes were opened. Lines were drawn in the sand.

SINS OF THE FLESH, by the way, are those things we do outwardly—sexual immorality, adultery, drunkenness, lying, cheating, stealing, rage, etc. Sins of the spirit are those characteristics that we inwardly harbor and hide—pride, unbelief, jealousy, hatred, or envy. Either will consume us. Both will distract us from loving God and convince us to love, protect, comfort, and exalt ourselves instead.

This brings me to the clean-cup theory.

One of my favorite campus visits was in the spring of 2005. In the middle of Indiana, I met a young man—the newly elected student-body president. No less than three times did we randomly bump into each other—first at the cafeteria, then in the bookstore, and finally while out walking across campus in between meetings. He was both energetic and magnetic. The funny thing about him was that he looked and acted very much like my own son.

At our third impromptu meeting he asked if I had read *The Calvary Road* by Roy Hession. I had not. He was adamant that I should read it, remarking that everything I talked about that morning in chapel was extremely similar to the words in this fifty-year-old, fifty-page book that he had chosen as one of his handbooks for life and ministry. He mentioned that he had read it three times. That in itself was intriguing to me. He was so convinced that I would love the book, he asked me to wait while he ran to his room to get a copy for me to read—that day!

So within the next few days I finished the book—for the *first* time. My young friend was right! I found much in this little handbook that encouraged me, especially the words of Joe Church, who said, "Revival is not when the roof blows off, but when the bottom falls out."

I was on a guided tour, it seemed! I was to continue in the "school of revival," and most interesting were the books that college students across America were giving me to read.

In Hession's book, there is an extensive discussion on the heart. He likens a person's heart to a cup—and describes it as being either dirty or clean.

Dirty cups are, of course, dull and dim and . . . dirty. Clean cups are shiny vessels ready for use. Hession simply challenges believers to live with clean cups—daily. Makes sense, doesn't it?

This isn't theological jargon. It is a practical application for keeping one's heart clean and right before God. It is the key, he says, to maintaining personal revival in your life.

*TODAY AND EVERY DAY, maybe two or three times a day, clean your cup. Honestly and transparently set your mind and body before God. Let Him into the depths of your heart . . . let Him confront you. Then come clean; confess all to Him . . . empty your cup completely and let Him fill you up to overflowing with an extra measure of His Holy Spirit.*

I had stumbled upon the concept myself twenty-two years earlier, when I made a decision of my will to confess my sins in writing to God every day. I begin with the verses from Psalm 139 that led me into honesty with God: "Search me, O God, and know my heart; test me and know my anxious thoughts. Point out anything in me that offends you, and lead me along the path of everlasting life" (vv. 23-24).

Not surprisingly, not one day has gone by when I did not have to clean my cup. But neither do I find it surprising that I have avoided great falls or swings or chasms in my walk with God. Neither have I wandered away—for more than a day—from loving God with all my heart.

The clean-cup method of daily confession and admission to God has saved my life—my witness. My fire for God, my passion to know Him more and invite others to enjoy His love, has grown brighter and brighter and hotter and hotter with each passing year.

Daily, honest, transparent confession in front of God every day is the way—the path—to safeguarding your soul. It is the practical method that leads to supernatural inner strength. God can always use—and is always looking for—a ready, clean cup. It is the way to keep one's inner furnace fired up, one's heart purified by fire!

If you suffer from a cold or dimly lit heart, you must clean the cup—and keep it clean—by asking God daily, if not hourly, to search your heart . . . to remove your sin, to right your relationships, to forgive your unbelief, to heal your body, to help you, to lift you, to strengthen your weaknesses, to empower you supernaturally, to repair your soul.

# holy AFFECTION

*The Holy Spirit gives the soul a natural relish for the sweetness of what is holy and for everything that is holy as it comes into view. He also intensifies a dislike and disgust of everything that is unholy.*

FROM *Religious Affections* BY JONATHAN EDWARDS

HE CAME UP TO ME—by himself. This wasn't one of those nights when many came forward to pray. But he did.

I had closed the meeting by saying that if anyone wanted me to be their janitor, I would wait for them in this spot. I chose the center step under a spotlight—I don't usually do that, but I did that night.

I just didn't get the feeling I had connected with too many that night. . . . The room was too big for the small group, the ceiling too high, the distance from me to the audience was too far to feel close. And I like to feel close—I like to look in people's eyes. I like to connect with each person in some way during a talk.

I had sat alone on the steps for quite awhile when he approached me.

A tall, thin surfer. That was my first impression anyway. He seemed a bit out of place. He didn't look like everyone else. He was shy—probably because many eyes were upon both of us. He told me his name was Nick.

Within seconds, the height and depth and length of the room diminished into the little circle of dim light on the car-peted steps where we were sitting. Nick sat one step below me, lowered his head, and began to share. "I'm done. I'm tired. I'm done getting into trouble, done using. I'm done. I don't want to do this life anymore. I want to believe that I can stop, that this craziness can end."

"OK, I believe it can stop tonight . . . I know it can," I said. I knew Nick's chase after unholy passions could end that very hour. I firmly believed what I was telling him—because it had happened for me. "Are you ready to turn and run the other way, to never look back?"

*"I CAN HAVE the resurrection life of Jesus here and now and it will exhibit itself through holiness."* —Oswald Chambers

Nick was surprisingly humble. And though I knew he was anything but innocent, his demeanor was not rebellious. He was in obvious emotional pain and personal shame. I could tell that he had quit loving the unholy long ago, and though it still had his affections . . . he was done chasing it. He hated his life.

"Would you like me to be your janitor?" I asked. Those words seem to encompass everything I want to say to someone who is so far from God. What an opportunity it is to take the heart and hand of those in as much need of a miracle as I was at that point in my life. What a privilege it is to pray with them, believing and knowing that God will change every aspect of their lives as much and as soon as they'll let Him.

Nick was indeed ready for a janitor. In essence, he was ready to dump the trash and filth from his heart and mind and be clean. I prayed for him, then he spent the next few minutes unloading his fears and failures in a simple but personal prayer to God.

Finally he looked up and said to me, "I'm going to get baptized tomorrow night. Will you go in the water with me?"

I had never been in the big, outdoor water fountain used for baptisms at this local church, but I thought *Why not?*

The next night's meeting was held in a tent. In the second row, Nick was seated with what appeared to be his entire family! I was a little surprised but really impressed that he seemed so determined to start his new life—immediately—and in front of so many who knew him so well.

I know firsthand what happens when a determined sinner goes to every length to mortify his sin, to die to his old self, and to make a public statement of his new faith: Power is released. Oh yes, real massive amounts of courage and strength and resolution are released in the one who is obsessed with the sacred and who publicly renounces the unholy passions of the past!

Immediately following the meeting, the baptism of those who wanted to make a public profession of faith took place.

The last time—and believe it or not—the only time I had ever baptized students occurred a few months earlier at the end of the first four-day Burning Hearts: Return to Revival. That was a joyous celebration with loud music, laughter, and cheers of a thousand onlookers.

This was different. Under the stars, outdoors, in cold, waist-high water, Nick went under, with his back braced by a pastor and myself. When he shot out of the water, there was only a broad, peaceful smile and a smattering of cheers from his family and friends.

BEGINNING AT FIVE O'CLOCK that night there was a twenty-four-hour prayer room available at the church. A classroom had been transformed into a prayer room by seven students from different schools and a college faculty member who were willing to spend hours preparing it to be set aside for meeting with the King.

As each of us took off our shoes before entering the room, we were greeted by a warm feeling, almost as if a cozy blanket was being placed around our shoulders as we passed from the outer hallway into this makeshift sanctuary. The only way to describe it was a physical feeling. The longer you were in there, the stronger the feelings of comfort and safety grew. God's presence became sweeter. You didn't want to leave.

The softly playing worship songs added just enough sound that no other voice could be heard. And even though one or more persons were in the room with you, you didn't talk to them; sometimes you caught their eye, but your focus was on the One you came to see and hear from. . . . No one else mattered.

*"ALL CHRISTIANS NEED MORE TEACHING in the art of prayer, and the Holy Spirit is the master teacher. The Spirit's help in prayer is mentioned in the Bible more frequently than any other help He gives us. All true praying comes from the Spirit's activity in our souls."*
—J. Oswald Sanders

I left the room around 2 a.m.—and by the 3 a.m. hour, at least fifteen students had visited the room, including Nick. Apparently, Nick asked a few girls to go to the prayer room with him that night . . . at about 3 a.m.

He had been captured fully and powerfully by the love of God. . . . He wanted to know God better, to spend time with Him. From what I heard, he visited the room several times during the twenty-four hours.

Nick—along with each one of us who entered the room—had a personal appointment with the King.

Whatever fear we came into the room with was gone when we left.

Whatever burden we carried when we entered the room was lighter when we left.

Whatever question we had as we stepped into the room was answered in some way, small or profound.

Some of us shed tears; others felt like singing or dancing.

Some of us found a corner to sit in and write and write and write . . . until our journals were full. Some of us couldn't stop smiling, and some of us could do nothing but sit still. Some of us pleaded with God for rescue. Others asked for forgiveness.

Nick is the classic example of most of us who have experienced God in a prayer room.

However you enter a place set aside for silent communication with God—with whatever stuff that has been in the way of hearing or seeing God—you leave different, changed. You will have a genuine affection—love—for God on your face and in your voice. You will have simply found your deepest longing is a holy person who has been waiting for you all along!

I was in awe of how many people visited the twenty-four-hour prayer room—writing names of loved ones with special needs on the paper that covered the walls, writing their favorite verses or creating some other artistic impression of this most moving corporate—yet individual—spiritual experience.

Nick, my new friend, was indeed chasing hard after God. He had turned his late-night energy and passion for adventure into pursuing the holy. And he wasn't disappointed. In fact, he became obsessed with God.

The next time I saw him was the next day, on a hill by the cross . . .

WHEN THE PRAYER ROOM CLOSED at five o'clock the next day, everyone who had visited the room was invited to meet at the top of a windy hill. We set up a sound system by a large, fifteen-foot cross overlooking much of Orange County and gathered to share stories and unite in prayer to close our seventy-two hours together—twenty-four of those hours spent in a prayer room with God. All agreed those who had entered the room would never be the same . . . because He had been there.

*"WHEN A TRUTH OF GOD is brought home to your soul, never allow it to pass without acting on it internally in your will. . . . Record it with ink and blood—work it into your life. The weakest saint who transacts business with Jesus Christ is liberated the second he acts and God's almighty power is available on his behalf."*
—*Oswald Chambers*

This closing time together was going to be brief and impromptu, so at the last minute, I looked around to ask someone to pray aloud. Nick caught my eye.

"Nick," I asked, "would you please close us in prayer?"

His face went from peaceful to pale. He was close enough for only me to hear his response: "I've never prayed out loud in public."

That didn't make a difference to me, so I motioned for him to take the microphone so we all could hear his prayer.

He stepped toward me, removed his baseball cap, and pushed the microphone back toward me, whispering, "I don't want to pray into a microphone."

I thought, *Oh well, most of us won't be able to hear him pray, but I'm sure it will be a fine prayer.*

When we all realized he was going to pray without further discussion, we bowed our heads, as if on cue. A most breathtaking, loud cry came out of this shy surfer boy's mouth. "Faaah-ther . . . !"

Chills raced through my body. I was so moved by the pleading sound in his voice that I immediately opened my eyes to look at him. He was looking up to the sky! I got an instant visual and emotional impression of what it might have been like to attend the ascension of Jesus.

Nick was expressing what we were all feeling. "You were there with us . . . now You're gone . . . we're going to have to do life without You in our safe, little prayer room. Show us how to keep You this near to us, this real to us!"

None of us will ever forget the longing or passion in Nick's voice. We knew that he had been with the Father— and so had we. Nick had been touched by the love of God. Nick showed us—in his innocence—how to pray with passion;

how to long for God with unbridled expression and call out to Him with fearless trust; how to chase after the sacred with the same passionate tenacity as many have to chase after the unholy.

I BELIEVE, AS JONATHAN EDWARDS TAUGHT, that "true religion" is both intensely practical *and* emotional. In fact, I've found few contemporary authors who encourage believers to live a holy life all day long, all year long, to the end of his or her life, even and especially persevering through any and all trials with an indomitable, unwavering obsession for the sacred. I cherish—and agree with—Edwards's contention that a "true Christian" (his words, not mine) will experience a continual change in nature and personality, hate evil and the appearance thereof, and reflect consistency and balance in all areas of life for all the days of his or her life.

Though a twenty-four-hour prayer room is a wonderfully transforming experience, you don't *need* a twenty-four-hour prayer room or even a revival meeting to feel the very real and powerful presence of the Lord, to hear His voice, to experience His touch . . .

You need only chase after the sacred . . .

with all your heart, body, mind, and soul . . .

today, now, this very hour.

He's here.

*AT EVERY MEETING, I never feel we should end at a specific time. I feel that God wants to meet with each person, and we will patiently wait for Him to do so—and He does! While we sing and pray and kneel and confess . . . it is as if He walks through the room and touches us, one at a time, until we've all been touched. And for those who stay to the very end, I always ask, "Why do you stay?" And I get the same answer every time: "Because He's here."*

A petite young girl in the front row began to dance. It was a dance I thought I might have seen before—as if it had been choreographed. But where would I have seen it?

I couldn't tell whether she was more noticeable because she didn't hide her bouncy, joyful moves or because she was in the front row. But she seemed almost to be jumping on springs.

Then it hit me. The dance steps were similar to cheerleaders' moves I had seen while coaching—she was making a series of victory motions with her arms while purposefully placing her feet in a repeatable eight-count pattern.

The meeting, in general, had been very, very low-key.

There had been no outwardly expressive or boisterous sing-ing—it had been rather mellow. Very few people had even lifted their arms in worship . . . so her dance seemed particu-larly special.

She had to be a very focused, very brave person to out-wardly and joyously express herself in dance to the Lord, in front of a very quiet group of 350 people. That is my only explanation, anyway. And if you were there . . . you might agree—there was just no other reason to dance. She wasn't joining in with others. She was alone, oblivious of the observ-ing crowd. She was freely directing her joy for the Lord in extremely pleasing-to-the-eye movement. She was absolutely radiant, unhindered, respectful, and simply unashamed to dance with her body, all the while exhibiting a most beautiful smile.

*"IT WILL REQUIRE a determined heart and more than a little courage to wrench ourselves loose from the grip of our times."*
—A. W. Tozer

I loved watching her! More than once, I was tempted to join her, but I didn't have the nerve! Yet, as she continued, her dancing made me smile. It really made me happy. As much as I wanted to dance with her . . . I could only watch in admiration.

ON MY SHORT AIRPLANE RIDE home the next day, I was often drawn to reflect upon the girl who so effortlessly and joyfully danced before the Lord. I eventually couldn't *stop* thinking about her.

So when I arrived home and found myself alone with just two hours to gather myself before I had to leave to speak again at four worship services over the next twenty-four hours . . . I turned on one of my favorite worship CDs by Crystal Lewis and went about unpacking, preparing a quick dinner, and gathering my notes and resources. But by the ninth song . . . I was standing up . . . then twirling, then *full-on dancing* in the living room, moving on into the family room, and swinging back through the kitchen.

And I'm not kidding . . . it was almost the very same "eight count" pattern as the young girl's dance.

I was smiling, dancing, twirling, laughing, lifting my arms, and singing very loudly . . . with my dog just staring at me . . . and this went on for quite a few minutes.

By the time I arrived at church that evening, I was fired up. My excitement for the Lord seemed combustible! I had just danced with the Lord, and I could not contain the fire that wanted to burst out of me. I remember telling a few friends that I felt like a fire thrower.

Afterward people described my presentation as filled with such a contagious passion that they could almost see and feel something streaming from me. At times during my talk, I got so choked up that I couldn't even speak. At other times, I was so overwhelmed with a desire for others to experience God's love that I talked too fast. And many times, I stretched out my arms to the walls or stood tall on my toes in order to physically demonstrate how wide and how high and how deep the love of God is . . .

I never told them I had danced with the King, but I had . . . and it was obvious to me that it had been exhilarating! Who, I wonder, would want to miss out on that kind of passion?

BY NOW, YOU REALIZE that I'm not theorizing about chasing after the sacred. I am speaking about a reality, about having a tangible relationship with God that doesn't take years to achieve.

If you're broken or beaten up,

    if you're stuck or stained,

        if you have a dead or dim heart . . .

I have the antidote for your misery. You can find relief for your madness in a moment—a moment of surrender.

I'm not exaggerating. It requires only a conscious decision of your will to turn—physically, emotionally, mentally, and spiritually—forever *from* the unholy and forever *toward* the sacred. Jesus said, "Do not love this world nor the things it offers you, for when you love the world, you do not have the love of the Father in you. For the world offers only a craving for physical pleasure, a craving for everything we see, and pride in our achievements and possessions. These are not from the Father, but are from this world. And this world is fading away, along with everything that people crave. But anyone who does what pleases God will live forever" (1 John 2:15-17).

There is only one choice if you want to possess the most sacred of obsessions. It is to reject and renounce any unholy cravings or passions. If you do so immediately, your life will change instantly for you as it did for me. But you must . . .

turn from,

give up, even

hate your unholy passions

to make room in your heart for the sacred.

How? With your body . . . run, turn, quit. With your mind . . . guard, protect, observe; always be alert and aware. With your heart . . . hate, kill, and mortify that which tempts, steals, and destroys the holy.

And keep doing those things. Every day, *every hour* if you need to . . . because the unholy is not going away, *it is not giving up on you*. It lives to consume you . . . you must reject and renounce it, now and forever.

Make it your obsession to chase *only* after the sacred, and you will catch Him.

AH. ANOTHER LIE WE BELIEVE——that the sacred is a thing, an *it,* a formula, a religion. No, the sacred is a Person. He is the holy One, the only One who can ever deeply and fully satisfy your soul. Oh, what a change occurs when we begin passionately chasing after . . . the Holy Spirit of the living God. J. Oswald Sanders, author of *Spiritual Leadership,* says, "Each of us is as full of the Spirit as we really want to be."

Why not make Him the object of your obsession?

*WHY NOT CHASE AFTER GOD with all of your heart, mind, and soul?*
*Why not?*

Why not emotionally release your love for God by lifting your hands and closing your eyes in worship or by pumping your fist in a victory cry? Why not express your joy for Him with dancing? (Try it at home, alone at first . . . and just see what it feels like.)

You know how to chase, how to dance, how to feel . . .

You feel excitement and passion when you sing favorite songs from the past or at the top of your lungs at a concert. You know how to hop, prance, jump, or dance when you hear your alma mater's fight song. You enjoy those

moments that take you to a place where you know you'll
feel deep joy or powerful excitement. You look forward
to the sporting events or entertainment venues where
you can release laughter or experience spirited victory
high fives. So why wouldn't you exhibit that same enthusiasm, passion, and joyous outward expression for the
Lord?

In *The Pursuit of God*, A. W. Tozer, a twentieth-century
pastor and author, makes a powerful case for apprehending
God. In 1948, he was a forlorn theologian, saddened by the
state of a lifeless, passionless body of believers. He wrote, "I
want deliberately to encourage this mighty longing after
God. The stiff and wooden quality about our religious lives is
a result of our lack of holy desire. Complacency is a deadly
foe of all spiritual growth. Acute desire must be present . . .
He waits to be wanted."

Tozer was adamant about passionately chasing after God.
He begged men and women to burn with zeal for God, never
to squelch the fiery urges that would drive us into the heart
of God. He pleaded with his readers never to relent, always
to push forward; to love God with our emotions and feelings
and personality . . . to follow *hard* after Him. At the very
least, Tozer wanted us to admire the freedom of others to
chase after, lift their hands up to, and dance with the living,
loving God.

Oh, won't you abandon your soul
  to the pursuit
    of the holy One?
Oh, won't you love Him with
  an outrageous passion,
    an extreme intensity to know Him more
      deeply,
      and an unrelenting fervor to remain true to
        Him above all others?

If you will chase after the sacred in this very hour, I am absolutely convinced you will both *discover* and *possess* the most unimaginable, overwhelming love and joy-filled passion you have ever felt.

A POPULAR REALITY TELEVISION SHOW in recent years focused on the passionate pursuit of one bachelor by up to twenty members of the opposite sex. In a controlled environment, the lone gentleman interviewed the assembled potential dates—with the hope that one of them might become his chosen mate. Each prospective bride vied for the hard-to-get attention and affection of the bachelor through a variety of group and one-on-one dates. All the while, TV voyeurs lived vicariously through the unconventional "find your mate" series.

The *best* date,

the *favorite* date,

the most *sought-after* date

was the one for which only one vying contestant was chosen
and awarded a special, private date with the bachelor. The
special date that would fulfill the desire of these women to be
with their beloved was affectionately dubbed "alone time."

*ALONE TIME—the key to knowing and loving another person?*

In the televised, nondate community segments of the
show, contestants complained, bickered, and strategized how
they might become the recipient of "alone time." They were
adamant that the most prized possession of the series was the
individual date with the bachelor, and the women fought des-
perately to obtain time alone with him for themselves. They
all knew it would ultimately set them apart from the crowd
and allow them to . . .

truly get to know the other person, and

become better known by the object of their affection!

So where am I going with this? In *Religious Affections,* Jonathan Edwards suggests that it is ridiculous to think you can
have endless zeal, undying loyalty, or exuberant passion
toward anyone you don't have the patience or desire to
spend time alone with . . .

If you were to consider your "alone time" with God as an

indicator of your desire to know Him better, how might you rate yourself? The words of a couple of authors of classic works on prayer not only convicted me, but motivated me to want to move away—far away—from my shabby state of prayerlessness. I'll never forget how wide my eyes opened and how quickly my jaw dropped the first time I read Leonard Ravenhill's quote, "No man is greater than his prayer life." At the time, I had *no* prayer life! O. Hallesby's comment, "Neglect prayer, neglect God," had a similar effect on me.

Do you jealously guard your alone time with God like one who is desperate to spend time with someone special? Do you look forward to spending time alone each day with God . . . to get to know Him better? Do you truly want to be known by God—or is that thought intimidating? The answers to these questions only scratch the surface. But if you are not hungry for time alone with God, you might ask yourself, *What is missing in my relationship with God that makes me not want to be near Him?*

*"PRAYER IS A CONVERSATION between two people who love each other." —Ros Rinker*

Much of my reading in the past two decades supports the conclusions I've formed from my personal experience.

Renowned authors, pastors, preachers, and missionaries from the last three centuries all affirm that spending time alone with God—defined as an individual, exciting, devoted, intentional, two-way, conversational appointment—is non-negotiable if you want to . . .

- stay connected to Him—with your emotions—for any length of time,
- sense His presence during both joys and trials,
- hear His voice as you read the inspired Word of God,
- experience the happiness of knowing and being known by Him, and
- be empowered to overcome the temptations of your flesh or the attacks by the enemy on your soul.

JONATHAN EDWARDS WROTE EXTENSIVELY on how to have an emotionally satisfying relationship with God—as if it was sought after by many, but missed by most! In *Religious Affections,* Edwards concludes that *true* Christianity will result in an intense, insatiable, spiritual longing or appetite.

I believe it is a relentless drive for "alone time" with God that makes spiritual giants out of mere men and women in every century. I also believe time alone with God is the secret to indomitable faith, desire for holiness, quiet inner strength, endless sobriety for strugglers, and deep joy on the journey of life.

Tozer, in the late 1940s, wrote his best known work, *The Pursuit of God*. A Chicago-area pastor, he was outspoken and fearless about the state of Christianity as he saw it at the time. He wrote, "We have been trying to apply machine-age methods to our relations with God. We read our chapter, have our short devotions and rush away, hoping to make up for our deep inward bankruptcy."

Tozer's challenges never stopped without describing how beautifully simple and incredibly accessible God's thoughts, presence, and power are for the average man or woman! He continued, "What God in His sovereignty may yet do on a worldwide scale, I do not claim to know. But what He will do for the plain man or woman who seeks His face I believe I do know and can tell others. Let any man turn to God in earnest, let him begin to exercise himself unto godliness, let him seek to develop his powers of spiritual receptivity by trust and obedience and humility, and the results will exceed anything he may have hoped in his leaner and weaker days." It does not take a mature, wealthy, or educated person to achieve this discipline of "alone time" with God—it just takes time and a willing heart.

Tozer discussed the fact that every saint in history was unique and responded to God in patterns true to his character and personality. Yet, he pointed out, every historic spiritual leader knew God, communicated with God, chased after God, could discern His voice . . . believed He existed, that He spoke and that He wanted their undivided attention, obedience, and worship. Tozer himself was relentless in describing the pursuit of God as . . . relentless.

*"I AM CONVINCED that to be filled with the Spirit is not an option, but a necessity. It is indispensable for the abundant life and for fruitful service. It is intended for all, needed by all, and available to all. That is why the Scripture commands us, 'Be filled with the Spirit.'"*—*Billy Graham*

For most of us—boomers, Xers, Yers—the thought of discipline, obedience, structure, prolonged silence, or unguided meditation makes us nervous.

Here is what *I think* makes us nervous: We instinctively know that forming new habits *in prayer* will change our thinking; it will remove any numbness. Time with God will break through any resistance, reluctance, or even rebellion *toward* God.

So how can those with an aversion to . . .

discipline,

quietness,

silence, or
> tuning out the noises of daily
> communication (for fear you might
> miss out on something)

form new habits that will usher them into the presence of the holy?

I suggest that you chase after the sacred with the very same passion and enthusiasm with which you have chased after the unholy! (Do we need to revisit the fact that each of us must address the unholy in our lives every day?)

Henri Nouwen, priest and teacher, wrote much about the path to prayer, calling it the "way of the heart." Because of the busyness and noise, even the responsibilities badgering each of us to yield to them, he said, "Precisely because our secular milieu offers us so few spiritual disciplines, we have to develop our own. We have, indeed, to fashion our own desert where we can withdraw every day, shake off our compulsions, and dwell in the gentle healing presence of our Lord."

He spoke of the sheer threat that awaited the minister who neglected to find, make, or fight for "alone time" with God. He said, "Without such a desert we will lose our own soul while preaching the gospel to others. But with such a spiritual abode, we will become increasingly conformed to him in whose Name we minister."

Nouwen doesn't convict the reader without giving

advice on how to daily acquire this desired discipline of "alone time." He continued, "The very first thing we need to do is set apart a time and a place to be with God and him alone. The concrete shape of this discipline of solitude will be different for each person . . . but a real discipline never remains vague or general. It is as concrete and specific as daily life itself."

I OFTEN MAKE SIGNIFICANT, lasting lifestyle changes when I'm fed up with myself.

I *always* make them when I'm ashamed of myself.

At the age of twenty-nine, I found myself a bitter, over-weight, angry . . . unhappy, unholy Christian. I didn't know then I had "hit bottom" or that freedom from my undisciplined character would require more discipline than I had ever exhibited in my entire life. But wondering *how* I would break through to change never really stopped me. Whenever I am willing to do *whatever* it takes to stop my sinful cycles—I break through!

Not to my surprise, God took the very next opportunity to show me the way to stay near Him—every day for the rest of my life.

I've got your attention now; I know I do. You want that kind of intimacy with God—the kind that is sustained day after day for the rest of your life. Listen carefully, for this proven method is not difficult, but it does require time and humility.

In February 1984, along with my husband and his youth ministry staff, I attended a yearly conference designed to equip youth workers for the next year of ministry. What I discovered was the power, purpose, and path to prayer . . .

It hadn't dawned on me to blame my numerous personality weaknesses, relationship problems, or character flaws on prayerlessness, so I didn't expect prayer to be the answer to them. But through a perfectly orchestrated series of messages designed to both convict and comfort this overworked, overweight, and overwhelmed wife, mother, and youth worker, God made it clear. If I wanted to return to the joy of my salvation, to be "happy in Jesus," I must not leave the convention as the same person who entered . . . undisciplined . . . lacking in prayer power. I must first admit that my prayerlessness—my lack of daily alone time with God—was negatively impacting absolutely everything I did or said or felt or thought!

At a final optional workshop on prayer, I stayed in my seat while everyone else exited the room . . . except for one other woman. She could tell I was upset—and I really was. But it wasn't a huge, obvious problem I was concealing—it was a huge, *not obvious* problem. What was the truth about my relationship with God? I was always too busy, too tired, or too lazy to spend time with Him. That negligence had wreaked havoc on every area of my life—which is another way of saying I hit bottom. At that point, without fanfare, I prayed out loud in front of one other person, "Lord, I make a decision to spend one hour a day with you for the rest of my life . . . "

*"PRAYER AND THE WORD are inseparably linked together. Power in the use of either is dependent upon the presence of the other."*
—*Andrew Murray*

One blustery Chicago Saturday afternoon, I made a simple decision in front of one other person in an empty hotel ballroom that has lasted over eight thousand days. . . . "Alone time" with God would be my highest daily priority.

DO YOU THINK I'M DIFFERENT than I was before I made that decision? Do you think that spending alone time with God for the last eight thousand days has changed me? Absolutely! But it may not be what you think.

*"SPEAK, LORD . . . let the romance begin!"* —*Oswald Chambers*

The greatest result of daily "alone time" with God is the joy, passion, fun, laughter, awe, wonder, excitement, compelling thoughts, and "aha" moments that occur every single time I meet with Him.

Spending time with God is not a duty. No one spends time with someone they love, admire, and want to know better because someone else makes them! That is a subtle lie . . . spending time with God is about loving Him and being loved by Him; wanting to know Him and be with Him.

*When you know you are loved by someone who knows the whole truth about you . . .*

*When you know someone special is waiting for you . . .*

*When you know that something wonderful or meaningful is going to happen every time you are alone together . . .*

*You don't need to be reminded . . .*

*You don't need to be shamed into meeting that person.*

*You rush, you run, you can't wait to meet.*

*You even begin to plan for your meetings!*

FOR A "NEWBIE" IN PRAYER to decide to pray for one hour a day for the rest of my life—without any track record to speak of nor a pattern in prayer which I knew to follow—was bold and scary. So I quickly rounded up and read every book with the word *prayer* in the title—well, *almost* every book! Most of the books were classics, often inexpensive (and usually written by dead people!).

After soaking up all the instruction I could find to teach me how to make prayer a practical part of my life, I came up with a number of ideas—tools and helps—that have made it easier for me to make prayer and alone time with God a regular part of my life.

How can you form new habits in prayer?

1. Plan your appointment with God *just one day in advance*.
2. Set your alarm clock for your appointment—this makes it real.
3. Record—journal—make commitments in writing.
4. Have a system for daily Bible reading—don't depend on yourself to do this.

I've included more ideas in the back of this book.

My husband, Roger, as a very young Christian, was challenged to read the Bible daily for just five minutes. He has done so for over thirty-five years of his life. It was a simple commitment that has formed the heart of a man after God—keeping him near God every day. We all need that, don't we? (By the way, Roger is the most Jesus-like fellow I've ever met. I equate his integrity with his willingness to sit under God's searchlight daily.)

*"THIS DESIRE TO PRACTICE the presence of God is the secret of all saints."* —*Richard Foster*

I DON'T PRETEND to think that a majority of us want to spend time with God in order to call ourselves—or even be known as—saints.

Frankly, the present reputation of Christians, at least in America, is not heralded by a saintly reference. But we *are* extremely needy of God's presence and power in our lives.

We've allowed culture to consume us and make us like it. The average Western Christian is much more like his culture than his God. Even now, over a majority (53 percent) of couples have decided not to stay married their entire lives; marriage is a devastated image of the essence of God's relationship with His church. Many Christians—ministers, married, single—are captivated by pornography, rather than by Jesus.

It's just the way it is . . . but it doesn't have to be.

We have become incredibly ineffective as children of the King—no longer considered by ourselves or others as a holy, set-apart people of the living, loving God.

But I am convinced that a swing in the opposite direction will be *immediate* if we stop neglecting our "alone time" with God as our primary source of strength, counsel, and conviction. I personally know this to be true. And it is called corporate revival when entire families, communities, cities, and nations return to God in humble prayer, confession, worship, and obedience to His written Word and Holy Spirit.

EVEN AS I PRESENT this chapter to you, I am a living testimony of one who has sought after God and found Him to speak to her through the most elementary pattern of daily conversation. I am not a saint but a sojourner. As C. S. Lewis said of himself, "As a fellow patient, having been admitted to the hospital a little earlier, I can give some good advice."

Over eight thousand hours with the living, loving God is proof . . . that He can take the most undisciplined, unruly, unworthy humans and meet with them every day for the rest of their lives!

If you want to sustain your passion for God . . .

If you want to form new habits in prayer . . .

If you want to be near God . . .

you must set aside time to be alone with Him!

It will require both time and discipline.

*"THE MAN WHO WOULD know God must give time to Him."*

*—A. W. Tozer*

One last thought . . . I think the weakest saints, like me, are the ones whom God calls to spend *more* "alone time" with Him. We need it; He knows it, and we know it! It's about time. It really is . . .

WHAT IS the Sacred Obsession?

The life-changing power of God.

The indwelling presence of God.

The passion of Christ.

The consuming, purifying fire of God.

The voice of God.

The Sacred Obsession is the Holy Person, the Holy Spirit of the living God.

IF, WITH EVERY PART of your body, mind, and soul, you will pursue,

even relentlessly chase after the Sacred Obsession,

until you capture a holy passion, you will experience

a refining fire, an unquenchable love, and

a dynamic and overcoming power . . .

washing over you—wave after wave.

I, like so many throughout the centuries, experienced an immediate and dramatic physical and moral transformation. The unexplainable presence of a holy God—in one hour—purged and purified me, then absolutely changed me into a new, radically different person than I was before.

Judging by the accounts others have written, my reaction to that experience was normal. Exuberant, zealous, passionate love for God and His Word, *not present the hour before,* instantly consumed my person and personality. The abrupt, profound moral changes, my newfound spiritual hunger and unrestrained desire to share my experience with others— even at the loss of friends and job—were not only sustained for days and months but have remained consistent and strong for over three decades.

What a fool I would have been to hold on to what enslaved me and refuse this pure love! And what I lost— those people and things I gave up to know and follow Christ— never loved me anyway.

Some would say I became a fanatic as I exhibited out-of-control, unusually ecstatic excitement to tell others about my encounter with God. Some thought I had been manipulated.

Perhaps the greatest proof that I possess the Sacred Obsession—a holy affection—happened in that moment when God entered my heart. Instantly, I *felt His love* and loved Him in return! And in that very same moment, I hated and turned from the addiction and immorality that had enslaved me for years. No hesitation, no fear, no doubt. This was real.

There is no other explanation. Nothing else can account for the powerful, purifying presence of the Holy Spirit in my life except that the Sacred Obsession, the Holy Spirit of the living God, invaded my person and personality and changed me . . . saved me.

This is the experience—well-documented for centuries—of those who have called themselves sinners, surrendered their entire wills to God, turned from their old lives, and invited the Person and power of the Holy Spirit to indwell them.

The day when Christ comes into your heart and fills you with His Holy Spirit is meant to be dynamic, passionate, and life changing! It is the moment, the realization that you are supernaturally empowered to no longer be the same. You are no longer destined for eternal death. You are no longer enslaved by sin. You are given a new life . . . and a new power to live that life! You are forgiven. You receive eternal life.

How can you respond to such an experience with any other emotion than relief, joy, tears, laughter, or amazement? Why not be ecstatic? You have experienced an unspeakable joy that comes from the deep, divine, undeserved forgiveness of a Holy God.

IT IS NORMAL to be excited about someone you love.

It is normal to be passionate.

It is abnormal, perhaps even a sign of trouble, if you are passive, bored, or unenthusiastic about your true love.

So why here, on earth, should your holy affection for the living, loving God *ever* fade or remain unexpressed? Who would it benefit for you to be reserved, unenthusiastic, or passionless about the most Sacred Obsession of your life? In fact, isn't that what everyone is searching for and chasing after—endless love, overwhelming joy, undeserved forgiveness, eternal life? In heaven, your gratitude to the Holy God will be eternal—you will worship Him forever. You will join throngs of angels who praise His name, acknowledging His power and glory forever and ever.

*GOD IS NOT PASSIVE in His love toward you. I see no reason, whatsoever, to be passive in your love toward Him.*

If you chase after Him, He will not only reveal Himself to you as the object of your deepest longing and heart's desire, but He will fill up to overflowing every emptiness! He will fall all over you with His love and presence. He wants to love you deeply. He will light your inner fire; He will warm your heart. He will quench your thirst. He will fill your hunger with Himself. He will immediately infuse you with all you need to exhibit discipline and courage. *He will enable you to do what you could not do before.*

You choose or refuse the Sacred Obsession.

You chase after or neglect the Sacred Obsession.

You invite or ignore the Sacred Obsession.

You embrace or avoid the Sacred Obsession.

Whatever you chase after, you become.

When your zeal and affection are directed toward the holy, you will become holy. You will find supernatural inner strength in God's divine energy flowing through you. You will exhibit unusual abilities that you (and others) know are not your own. You will be satisfied.

And this, of course, will be your sign, your proof that you are obsessed with the sacred.

I beg you to relinquish, with one final act of confession, the unholy things that rule your life and resolve *never to look back longingly* on your unholy passions. Then pursue with your wildest passion and wholehearted affection . . . the holy One. There you will find the most sacred obsession of your life.

But don't stay there too long without going out to tell others where He may be found . . . what He is really like . . . how much He loves . . .

He is waiting for you to tell them about your Sacred Obsession.

*THERE IS ONLY ONE holy passion. There is only one Sacred Obsession.*

# alone
# time
## WITH GOD

*We fool ourselves if we think that such a sacramental way of living is automatic. We must desire it and seek it out. We must order our lives in particular ways. We must take up a consciously chosen course of action that will draw us more deeply into perpetual communion with the Father.*

FROM *Freedom of Simplicity* BY RICHARD FOSTER

OVER TWENTY-TWO YEARS AGO, I developed a prayer note-book and called it *My Partner Prayer Notebook*. It has two parts. In my part I *talk to God* and in God's part, I *listen to Him*.

In the first part of my alone time, I *talk to God* by journal writing my prayers of *Praise, Admission, Request,* and *Thanks.* In the second part, I *listen to God* by recording His thoughts to me in the following sections: *Listening, Messages, New Testament, Old Testament, Proverbs,* and *To Do.*

How I originally determined which four types of prayers I would pray during my hour is anyone's guess, but it was years later that I understood the pattern that leads me to begin my conversations with God by rereading, rewriting, and paraphrasing the Psalms is certainly not a new idea! Written prayer is the entire context of the book of Psalms. It is where prayer has been recorded to teach believers—for centuries—*how to pray and worship!*

Not even once had I read through the book of Psalms when I began to pray an hour a day. Now, over two decades later, it is the most worn, well-read book of my Bible. The Psalms connect me to God. As I paraphrase them, I tell God in my own words how much I love Him, how much I need Him, how dependable and awesome and strong and powerful and wonderful He is!

The **Praise** section of my prayer time sets the tone for

my entire hour in prayer—I walk away saying, writing, believing that my God is all I need. By following the Psalms, 1–150, I see the futility in worry, fear, or doubt . . .

By paraphrasing the Psalms, I daily tell God, "You are mine. I trust you. I am yours. You are all I need!" My identity—and His identity—are clearly recorded in writing every day. I find it to be a most powerful way to enter into "alone time" with God.

Again, the uniqueness of my prayer format would lead me from praising God to admitting to Him that I was struggling, battling, or being tempted. I had not initially calculated a profound reasoning behind the order of Praise, Admit, Request, and Thanks. But in hindsight, it is amazing how important confession is to, for, and by believers—in preparing them to be fully effective in their prayer lives! I have found that it is not just the concept of daily confession and admission that is critical, but taking the action step of confessing my sins in writing that has taken my character to the greater depths of cleansing!

Since the very beginning of my "alone time" with God, it seemed very natural for me to talk to Him about everything. But the regular, daily practice of confessing my sins in writing starts with a simple verse that I write down just as I move from the Praise to the **Admit** section. Daily, I simply picture myself sitting across from Jesus, and I begin to write out the words of Psalm 139:23-24: "Search me, O God, and know my heart; test me and know my anxious thoughts. Point out anything in me that offends you, and lead me along the path of everlasting life."

Not one day has gone by where I've said to God, "Hmm . . . I can't think of *any* area of my life that does not need attention, where I'm not struggling, where I'm not fighting against my sin nature or battling to push away temptation from my heart. No, nothing to discuss today . . ."

Never! I always have a heart-to-heart discussion with God that takes me right to a place of confession—honest, transparent admission.

I love the concept of having an ongoing, personal— never ending—revival! Roy Hession believed the way to sustain continuous, personal revival was experienced in "immediate obedience to the Holy Spirit." The act of daily confession of sin to God—in writing—is the most practical way I have discovered to keep my "cup clean" every day, to come under the searchlight of the Holy Spirit, and to sustain continuous revival in my personal life! Hession's definition of revival says it all: "Revival is simply you and I walking along the highway in complete oneness with the Lord Jesus and with one another, with cups continually cleansed and overflowing with the life and love of God."

Sounds fabulous, doesn't it? No pretending, hiding,

excusing, or blaming others for the areas in life with which you struggle. Taking our "stuff" daily to God, asking Him to counsel us, purge us, and remove the excuses, lies, and secret habits from our lives *is the link* to continuous, personal revival.

You don't need to pay a counselor to tell you what the Lord will gladly, gently tell you . . . though you may need to pay one to help you *implement* God's marching orders. But if you ask the Lord to search you . . . He will. And He will give you courage; He will show you the way of escape. He will. You must act, though, as if you believe what it says in 1 John 1:9: "If we confess our sins, He is faithful and just to forgive us our sins, and to cleanse us from all unrighteousness" (KJV).

The great benefit of . . .

a clean cup,

a life that is in continuous, personal revival,

a life that is day-by-day walking with God,

is to live a life that is full of power, inspiration, and the Holy Spirit! The life of one who is walking in the light with God is best described by Nouwen, who writes, "To live in a state of ongoing preparedness so that, when someone who is drowning in the world comes into your world, you are ready to reach out and help."

The pattern in prayer makes even more sense . . .

After I confess my sins in writing, I move to the

**Request** section of the notebook. The freedom released after transparent and honest conversation with God regarding my character flaws or shortcomings is found in James 5:16, "The earnest prayer of a righteous person has great power and produces wonderful results."

When I am daily humble and broken before God, I can receive forgiveness and a fresh wind on my fire. I am filled with a power to intercede for others, as well as courage to ask for personal intervention. In Psalm 84:11, I am reminded that "the LORD will withhold no good thing from those who do what is right." And in Psalm 66:18, I read that "if I had not confessed the sin in my heart, the Lord would not have listened."

After personal confession each day, with great conviction and a clean conscience, I pray for my husband, son, family members, pastors, political leaders, the sick, the struggling, those in need . . . confidently laying my requests before God and waiting in expectation for His answers.

My Request list is long! I write down every name . . . not only so I don't forget to pray for others, but so I can *see* God's answers to prayer!

The Request section of my prayer notebook is also a place to report to the Boss (or to the General); as Nikos Kanzantzakis described in *The Saviors of God: Spiritual Exercises,* "My prayer is the report of a soldier to his general: This is what I did today, this is how I fought to save the entire battle in my own sector, these are the obstacles I found, this is how I plan to fight tomorrow."

Prayer is not passive.

Prayer is not boring.

Prayer is not insignificant.

Prayer is powerful.

Prayer is interactive.

Prayer is life changing!

Leonard Ravenhill wrote volumes on prayer. Many of his findings took years for me to validate, but with this I *finally* agree: "The people who pray most accomplish most!"

Next, I write a thank-you note to God in the **Thanks** section of *My Partner Prayer Notebook* every day. Appreciation . . . we all love it. We all want it. We miss it when we don't get it. We need it. And so does God! To recognize, in writing, what He said to you, how He met your need, to acknowledge that He noticed your tear . . . is priceless—to both of you.

Then I listen to God through a planned "listening" system that encourages me to hold on, to be patient, to wait for Him, to stop, or to go in another direction. I always know He is listening.

Listening to God, for me, proves that God exists—it is the place where my faith is grounded, developed, and strengthened. Oswald Chambers wrote, "For every detail of common sense in life, there is a truth God has revealed by which we can prove in our practical experience what we believe God to be."

As I listen to God daily, He proves Himself to me. His voice, His thoughts, His promises, His words are worth living and fighting for . . . staking one's life upon.

In the "Listen to God" part of my notebook, I divide the experience into 6 sections: L, M, N, O, P, and To Do.

In the **Listen** section, my pastor/husband has taught me just to write down what I think and feel God is saying to me today. God's thoughts to me will never be in contradiction to the Word of God, so over time, the Listen section becomes a part of God's instruction and confirmation to me. God's thoughts to me are not always sweet words, either. Often they are ideas and promptings that require my willingness (we could call it obedience) to call, send, write, ask, forgive, make amends . . . you know those thoughts!

Albert Edward Day, in *The Captivating Presence,* wrote, "Obedience is indispensable. But obedience to God, who is present with us in every situation and is speaking to us all the time . . . quickens our sensitivity to Him and our capacity to understand Him and so makes more real our sense of His presence."

Those moments where a simple thought pierces our

soul, sends chills up our spine or heat to our cheeks . . .
those are the thoughts that don't go away, that make sense,
that sound like a sincerely concerned parent; they are wise
and true and relentless. You know those thoughts. The Listen section of my notebook is a written record of those
thoughts. They are consistent, powerful, personal, and often
require *my* response of obedience.

The **Message** section of *My Partner Prayer Notebook* is
another place—just one more confirmation—where I record
the messages of pastors, authors, or teachers who instruct me
through the Word of God. Writing down the verses they use
almost always confirms something God has been saying to my
heart. They often convict me in a way that will move or moti-
vate me. For over two decades, I have taken notes during ser-
mons; I just don't want to miss—or forget—what God is
saying to me.

The next three sections of the "listen to God" part
include reading from the New Testament, Old Testament,
and Proverbs each day. This pattern began with my notebook
system twenty-two years ago and was quickly sustained with
the design of a 365-day Bible—I use the *Change Your Life
Daily Bible,* a special edition of the *One Year Bible.*

I've read the Bible daily for almost twenty years in a
row . . . and from cover to cover . . . not because I'm a theologian or a pastor or because my church has asked me to do

so, but because *this is where God speaks to me every day*! In fact, Martin Luther wrote about the Bible as more than a voice calling out to us. He said, "The Bible is alive! It speaks to me; it has feet; it runs after me; it has hands; it takes hold of me."

It is A. W. Tozer who suggests that today's Christians are hearing impaired because they are victims of divided psychology, able to accept the Bible as the Word of God, but unable to believe "the words on the page are actually for them"! He begs us to "wait on God . . . get alone, preferably with our Bible outspread before us. Then if we will, we may draw near to God and begin to hear Him speak to us in our hearts."

The final section of *My Partner*—the **To-Do** section—is as important as any of the other sections. It is the place where I transfer the thoughts and ideas and "marching orders" that I receive during my hour of prayer onto my daily calendar (or To-Do list). Oswald Chambers, in his daily devotional *My Utmost for His Highest,* writes, "When a truth of God is brought home to your soul, never allow it to pass without acting on it internally in your will . . . record it with ink and with blood—work it into your life. The weakest saint who transacts business with Jesus Christ is liberated the second he acts and God's almighty power is available on His behalf."

The step of doing what you hear God ask you to do is obedience, right? Many of us talk to God but never listen.

Some of us pray with great intention but never follow through with the ideas and promptings that occur during our time in prayer—perhaps because we have not written them down? (Yet we are a nation full of electronic calendars, e-mails, and saved computer documents.)

Whether we are just forgetful or purposely avoiding God's promptings by procrastinating, if we don't immediately act upon what God asks of us during daily appointments with Him, we miss out on the most powerful result of prayer—answers! Charles Stanley once said, "Don't pray about anything you wouldn't want God to do through you!"

In fact, Jonathan Edwards had a Nike-esque approach to God. He wrote, "So godliness consists not merely in having a heart intent on doing the will of God, but having a heart that actually does it."

It is in your power to make your alone time with God the most important, nonnegotiable, exciting, rewarding appointment on your daily calendar. *Just do it!*

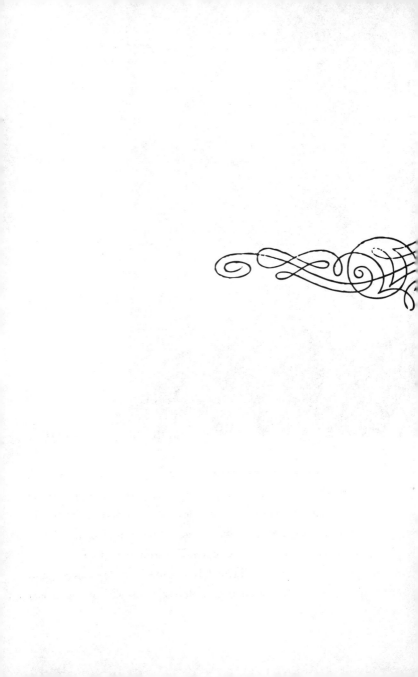

# about THE AUTHOR

BECKY TIRABASSI has been sharing her story at conferences, churches, and colleges since 1976. After almost two decades as a writer and speaker in youth work, Becky began a multimedia corporation, Becky Tirabassi Change Your Life, Inc. In 1996, she began to reach men, women, and students with her life-changing message through radio, television, resources, and events. Her many opportunities to reach people include having been a guest contributor on CBS's *The Early Show,* the host of the *Change Your Life Daily Radio Minute,* an occasional guest on *Focus on the Family* with Dr. Dobson, and a speaker with Women of Faith and Youth Specialties, as well as sharing her story in her hometown at the 1994 Greater Cleveland Billy Graham Crusade.

In 2005, Tirabassi founded a student organization, Burning Hearts, Inc. Surprisingly, after almost a decade away, she has returned to speaking for students across America, as well as adults, and she is passionate about calling them to be sold out to prayer, set apart in purity, and sent out with purpose.

To reach Becky Tirabassi or for more information on events or resources, contact

BECKY TIRABASSI CHANGE YOUR LIFE, INC.
BOX 9672
NEWPORT BEACH, CA 92660
1-800-444-6189
WWW.CHANGEYOURLIFEDAILY.COM

*or*

BURNING HEARTS, INC.
BOX 10926
NEWPORT BEACH, CA 92658
1-949-644-7466
WWW.THEBURNINGHEARTCONTRACT.COM

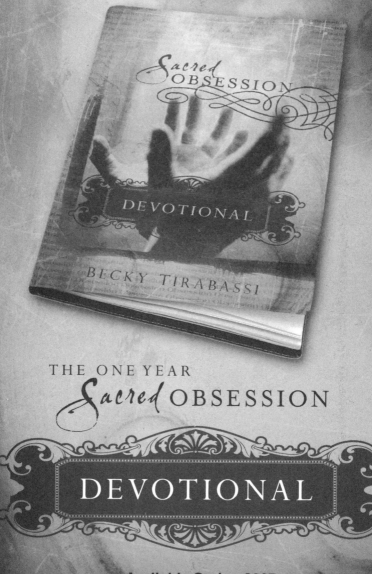

**COMING SOON!**

THE ONE YEAR *Sacred* OBSESSION

## DEVOTIONAL

**Available Spring 2007**

hange Your Life Daily Bible

Change Your Life Daily Journal

# Keep the Change

Let Prayer Change Your Life

The Burning Heart Contract

My Prayer Partner Notebook

ransform Your Game *(with Roger Tirabassi)*

The Front Nine *(with Roger Tirabassi)*

# download

## FREE AUDIO CLIPS
## OF BECKY SPEAKING

www.changeyourlifedaily.com